DESTINED
for GRACE

Mitch Poulin

DESTINED
for GRACE

Walking in God's Plan for Your Life

TATE PUBLISHING
AND ENTERPRISES, LLC

Published by Tate Publishing & Enterprises, LLC
127 E. Trade Center Terrace | Mustang, Oklahoma 73064 USA
1.888.361.9473 | www.tatepublishing.com

Tate Publishing is committed to excellence in the publishing industry. The company reflects the philosophy established by the founders, based on Psalm 68:11,
"The Lord gave the word and great was the company of those who published it."

Book design copyright © 2013 by Tate Publishing, LLC. All rights reserved.
Cover design by Junriel Boquecosa
Interior design by Jomar Ouano

Published in the United States of America

ISBN: 978-1-62746-590-8
1. Religion / Christian Life / Spiritual Growth
2. Religion / Christian Theology / General
13.06.20

CONTENTS

PREFACE

God tells us that He has revealed Himself to us through His creation (Rom 1:20). When we consider the awesome beauty, harmony, and splendor of creation, we cannot help but know God and His sovereign power and majesty. We can know of God through creation, but we cannot know God unless He reveals Himself to us. God uses the physical distance between the heavens and the earth to describe how much higher His thoughts and ways are above ours (Isa 55:8–9). Mankind on our own lacks truth, mercy, and the knowledge of God, so any of our attempts to worship God apart from His revelation (the Bible) is in vain (Hos 4:1, 6; Matt 15:9).

When God brought His people out of slavery in Egypt, He gave His servant Moses the understanding of Himself and His ways (Rom 3:1–2; Ex 24:3). God instructed Moses to write down His words so the people of God could always know Him and live their lives as He wanted them to (Deut 6:4–9, 11:18–21; Isa 59:21; Matt 4:4). God's desire was for His word to be passed down from generation to generation;

that parents would talk of Him to their children, teaching them daily. God tells us to hold onto His word; to keep His word in our hearts. We are to live by every word that proceeded from the mouth of God. At the time when Moses gave God's people His word, they all agreed to follow it (Ex 24:3). Throughout history, God has spoken to His people through His prophets, Jesus Christ, and the followers of Jesus Christ that spent time with Him (Heb 1:1–2; Luke 24:27; Amos 3:7; 2 Peter 3:1–2). God's word didn't come from anyone's private interpretation nor did it come by the will of man, but was given to us by God through people He chose (2 Tim 3:16; 2 Peter 1:20–21). Even the words Jesus spoke came from the Father (John 17:8). Jesus took what God gave Him and passed it on to His followers. They in turn wrote them down for all of us to benefit from. God's inspired word teaches us about Him and provides us with direction for our lives (Rom 15:4). So you can see that God teaches us about Himself and how to live our lives in alignment with Him through His spoken word written down for us in the Bible by people God chose.

God tells us that He gives wisdom, knowledge, and understanding through His spoken word (Pro 2:6–7). The Holy Spirit opens our hearts and reveals God's word to us so that we can comprehend and understand spiritual matters (Matt 16:17; Luke 24:45; Acts 16:14; 1 Cor 2:13–14). Over the ages, many have desired to know the things that God reveals to us today through the Bible (Matt 13:16–17). God has put forth His word for all generations to have, yet He only reveals the meaning of His word to those He chooses, and the rest He hardens (Ps 102:18; Matt 13:10–15). That's because mankind has rejected God and His word. Even Israel, the people God chose to reveal Himself to, quickly turned from God and went their own way. That's our MO isn't it? We want to go our own way apart from God. We want to decide for ourselves what is right and what is wrong. We don't like having a God that requires faith, so we make images and idols to worship rather than worshipping the one true God. Therefore, God at this time is only revealing Himself to people He has a specific purpose for—to those He is calling to Himself.

God leads those He is calling by His word (James 1:18). When we receive the word of God, we receive it as the truth of God and not man's word (1 Thess 2:13). That's really the measuring stick for knowing if God is calling you. Regardless of where you've been in your life spiritually or where you are now, when you start desiring to know God and look to His word as truth, God is probably drawing you near to Him. As we read His word and grow in understanding, we hold onto and obey the words He's given us because we're developing a love for God and Jesus Christ (John 8:31–32). By doing so, God's word becomes effective in our lives (1 Thess 2:13). God comes to us and makes His home within us, blessing us with eternal life (Luke 11:28; John 5:24, 6:63, 14:23–24). Those that God has given understanding to should never glory in their understanding, but recognize that true wisdom is having a relationship with God and knowing that wisdom comes from God (Jer 9:23–24). God's spoken word goes forth and accomplishes His will in those He chooses to accomplish it through (Isa 55:11).

When Jesus was being tried before Pilate just prior to His scourging and crucifixion, Jesus told Pilate that He came into the world to bear witness to the truth. Pilate then responded by asking, "What is truth?" (John 18:37–38). That seems to be the overriding question for society, isn't it? What is the truth, and where do we find it. We all have opinions. Many think that truth is relative; that truth for you may not be truth for me. We live in a society where "spin" has become the norm and the only absolutes we hold to come from science. However, for those of us whom God is drawing to Himself, the only source of spiritual truth comes from the Bible because God tells us that His written word to us is truth, and we believe (Ps 119:142; Dan 10:21; John 17:17).

God's word is living and powerful. It is sharper than a two-edged sword that cuts through any deception or lies, discerning the thoughts and intent of our hearts (Heb 4:12; Eph 6:17). God warns us not to add to or take away from His word (Deut 4:2). He tells us that the grass withers and the flowers fade, but His word stands forever (Isa 40:8). Heaven and earth will pass away but God's word will remain (Luke 21:33).

God's word is the foundation for this book. Every thought and idea written down comes from the Bible. This work organizes and assembles God's plan for mankind in a manor that is easy to follow but remains true to what God's word tells us. My heart's desire in writing this work was to not speak from my own understanding, but to allow the scriptures as given to us by our all powerful God tell the story.

INTRODUCTION

There are so many stories of loved ones who die before giving their lives over to God or even having the chance to know God. Often, these circumstances of life become the basis for rejecting God or refusing to believe there is a God. We've all heard stories of children who die at a young age. Are they saved? Will God somehow reveal himself to them? What about people who die never hearing about God or Jesus Christ, or for that matter, what about all the people born prior to the time when Jesus Christ walked the earth? Are they lost? If God is so powerful, why does knowing Him and having a relationship with Him seem to be a matter of chance? What about the family that desperately tries to save their dying mother or father only to have them die without accepting Jesus Christ as their Lord and Savior? The family is left grieving for their loss and trying to come to terms with the fact that their parent is lost. What about those committing suicide? Are they lost? Will they be rejected even though their lives were spinning out of control and ending their lives became the only viable option they could rationalize in their state of mind? What about people born in cultures where their religion is not Christianity—people whose belief systems are so intertwined with their ancestors that they cannot change? If they embrace Christianity, they must accept the fact that their relatives are lost forever. How do they see God as loving and caring, yet He has rejected their ancestors?

Over and over again, I hear very converted people—people who know the scriptures and have a close relationship with God reconciling the dilemma this way: "I know God is a God of love, so I believe that it's a mystery we can't solve, yet I know God will take care of them." This explanation is usually given for young children who die and privately thought about family members dying without having a relationship with God. We experience God's love in our own lives, so we know God must have a plan for these lost people, yet our doctrine or beliefs don't allow for such exceptions. We know in our heart that we are really no different than the people who are lost except for the fact that God thankfully and wonderfully drew us to Himself. When I have these types of discussions, I find that I have to be very cautious about going too far with my views. Christians need to maintain a stable foundation from God's word, so discussions that are outside doctrinal norms are off-limits for some of us. Fair enough. Besides, I was never prepared to lay everything I was learning in front of them to show a different light on the scriptures.

There's also the reality that God has to call us to Him in order for us to even seek Him. The Scripture is very clear on this. Over and over again, the Scriptures reveal that the servants of God were selected by God for a specific purpose God had for them. Most of us have seen this in our own lives—how we didn't really want a relationship with God, yet it was evident that He was drawing us to Him. We start off not even considering a relationship with God. We're young and invincible; we don't need God in our lives. We're full of knowledge and want to form our own beliefs, so we question if God really exists like our parents keep trying to persuade us of. We're going our own direction. When God calls us, He uses our pride to bring about circumstances that drive us to our knees. It's then that God reveals Himself to us. We've reached bottom, so we cry out for His help. Rejecting God and going our own way has brought us to ruin, so we turn to God in shame and ask for His forgiveness. God's calling was not something we initiated. We can't even take credit for turning to Him because He provided everything we needed to make the change. I guess if we want to own any part of our calling, it's the ruined state we put our lives in apart from God.

In the book of John, Jesus stood up during a Jewish feast and invited anyone who thirsts to come to Him. He told the crowd that those who believe will be given the gift of the Holy Spirit (John 7:37–39). Jesus used the analogy of being thirsty and then given a drink to refresh our body to explain how those who are spiritually *thirsting* will be renewed by God's Spirit. Jesus invited anyone who thirsts! Really? We know that God's calling provides the *thirst* in us, yet we don't see God drawing all men to Himself today. Was Jesus telling the crowd that this would happen then, or was He referring to some future time? Those who try to sell us on the idea that God has provided a means for all mankind to come to Him today must somehow explain how such an all powerful God is constrained by time and chance. That people who have never been exposed to Jesus Christ are condemned to an eternity apart from God. This is not just a few people. This is millions and millions of people that have never been given the opportunity to know our Lord and Savior.

Clearly, God is only drawing a small number of people referred to in the Bible as a remnant or the *first fruits of the Spirit* to Himself now. But how can this be? If God isn't drawing all men to Himself today, are all those He's not drawing lost? Did God truly create them for destruction? What is the fate of all those people who are not being called by God today?

I know personally that our Creator God is a God of love and that He sent His Son to die for me so that I may be with Him. I didn't want it or deserve it, but thankfully God knew better. In the core of my being, I don't see God as disconnected with the future of His creation as we typically portray Him in the church today. I also recognized that as a church, our understanding of God's calling, predestination, and our gift of choice were incomplete and didn't fully align with what God's word was telling me. These issues drove me to search the Scriptures from Genesis to Revelation looking for the answers. This book is the result of that study.

My desire is not to convince anyone of my beliefs. We all know that God reveals Himself to each of us in unique ways as His Spirit leads us. God requires that we be true to the understanding He has convicted us of. I do present Scripture in a very determined order and ask questions that lead down a particular path. However, it's between you and God how you will perceive and internalize each passage. Some will reject the fundamental basis for writing this and thus reject this message. That's okay if that's where God is leading you. Some will not agree with the conclusions I come to, yet there will be questions left as to what God's plan really is. Keep questioning, but always turn to Scripture and prayer to find God's answer for you. Some will agree yet cannot embrace what the Scriptures are saying because of cultural or religious bias. I want to encourage you to look deeply into God's love for answers.

I was a member of a church that changed their fundamental way of viewing grace. It tore the church apart. I found myself somewhat lost because I believed that their former teaching on grace was Biblically based and foundationally sound. How was it that I had listened to the teaching of the church, relied on God's Spirit living in me to lead me, studied God's word to confirm the teaching, and believed that it truly was God's way, yet somehow I was wrong? God used this event to help me recognize that I can have pride in my knowledge when I become too dogmatic. He also used this event to deepen my understanding of His grace and help me recognize that He allows our understanding of Him and His plan for mankind to be incomplete, yet His desire is for us to keep searching for Him, and be open to new revelations from Him.

God also showed me that I need to have compassion on other Christian beliefs. The thinking goes like this: the Holy Spirit lives in me, revealing the truth of God to me so when I read something in Scripture and it connects with other scriptures and aligns with my church teaching, then I know it's absolutely true. This thinking is true to a point, and as I stated earlier, God does expect us to be committed to what He has revealed to us. The problem comes when our doctrine doesn't match perfectly with other Christian's doctrine. God has brought those people who are every bit as convicted of their truths from the Bible to a different place than us. We should be able to learn and grow from each other. Instead, too often these doctrinal differences build walls between us and other Christians, or we become blinded to spiritual growth by dogmatically defending our understanding and not considering the understanding God has given to other Christians. I feel compelled to ask the question, why do we need so many denominations? Or for that matter, why do we need any denominations? To the unbeliever observing Christian behavior, do these separations we have really bring glory to God? Or maybe the better question is, how can our differences become a way for the church to grow and truly bring glory to God?

Finally, there are some who will see the Scriptures as I see them and find joy and encouragement in God's amazing love for mankind. Praise God! I find that having this truth has caused me to stop squabbling over doctrine. I've been set free from the bondage of doctrine and now focus on drawing closer to God and showing love for my fellow man. It's also opened the Scriptures up to me in ways I never imagined before. God's plan for all mankind truly is amazing.

Let me start by saying I absolutely hold to all the basic doctrines of the church. Specific to this discussion, I believe that God tells us there will be a resurrection of all mankind— those saved to eternal life and those who reject Jesus Christ and His sacrifice for their sins to judgment and everlasting punishment. The Bible is very clear; it states over and over again, in many different ways that the wicked will perish. There is no questioning this law God has set in motion. It's kind of like gravity. If you jump off a building, you're going to fall. It's a law that no one can change or overcome. However, there are two thoughts that are woven into the fabric of our beliefs that cause confusion. The first misunderstanding we have is thinking that a restored relationship with God must come before we die. This idea is nowhere stated in the Bible but has become a part of our understanding because we don't fully understand God's plan, so we default to the physical constraints of this life. The second misunderstanding we have is related to the nature of God's judgment. Traditionally, we view the judgment as an event—the wicked are raised, sentenced, and tossed into hell. Scriptures will be presented to show that God's judgment is not an event but rather a period of evaluation, just as those who are followers of Christ today are being evaluated or judged. Scriptures related to these two issues will be thoroughly discussed, but my ultimate purpose is to show through Scripture what God's will for all mankind is.

Eternal judgment is real for anyone who rejects God. God put the desire to live eternally in us, but none of us has eternal life apart from God. God is the only source of life, so rejection of Him is rejection of life. God's spirit living in us gives us life so how can we even think to live apart from God? God has allowed this arrogance in us to teach us what life becomes when we do things our own way, but God will not allow this childish thinking to remain. God warns us about eternal judgment and the dangers of continuing to try to live apart from Him, but His desire is that we never go there. The Bible is full of eternal judgment warnings for the wicked, but God's intention, His desire for us is that every one of us heeds

His warnings and never goes to that place. I'd like to use a simple example from my life to explain the idea.

When my oldest son was born, we lived on a busy street. From the time my son was old enough to walk, we started teaching him about the road—how dangerous it was to be in the front yard, that he had to stay in the backyard, and there would be consequences if he wandered beyond the back corner of the house to the side of the house. Every single time he was outside, we would watch over him (we didn't have a fenced in area), and even if he got close to the corner of the house, we would begin our coaching and alerting him to the dangers. On a day that is burned into my memory, I was responsible for watching my son. It seemed like my eyes were off him for only a few seconds, and I realized he was headed for the road. I instinctively ran toward him, yelling for him to stop, but that just made him think I was chasing him, and being the strong-minded toddler he was, that made him run even more fervently toward the road. At that point, I realized I would not catch him in time, so I stopped and yelled out a shriek for him to stop now! He froze in his tracks. I slowly walked toward him, sternly telling him to come toward me. He didn't budge. He just looked at me with a look that told me he wasn't bought into this whole danger thing, but he would comply for the moment. When I was close enough, I lunged for him and pulled him close into my arms. I was angry, thankful, scared, and broken for my lack of attention, yet rejoicing because my son was safe. God had frozen him in his tracks, and I was able to get to him three feet from the road and all the traffic of rush hour whizzing by.

The danger of the road was real. The continual disciplining of my son was there to keep him from going into the road. My heart's desire was for him to never go into the road, but I knew that if left on his own, he would go there. So I put fear in him, I disciplined him, and I coached him all with the intention that he would never actually go into the road. The fact that he didn't go into the road doesn't mean that the danger wasn't there; it was.

The same is true of the final eternal judgment for the wicked. It's there, and it's real, but God's will is that no one would ever go there. The difference between my experience with my child and God's plan to restore His relationship with all mankind is that I'm human with human flaws and weaknesses, while God is perfect, and His plan is perfect. It wasn't my effort that was responsible for saving my son's life. It was God looking over him and me that saved him. However, God is in control of His plan to draw us back to Him. He knows each of us better than we know ourselves. He knows all our thoughts. He knows what it will take for each of us to drop to our knees and call out to Him for help. He is providing everything we need to turn to Him, and we all will turn to Him.

A good friend once said that without God's judgment, we wouldn't understand His grace. In other words, if there weren't people who are going to receive God's eternal punishment, we wouldn't appreciate God saving those who believe in Jesus Christ. This is true to a point, but what's missing in this view is God's tremendous love for us. We are all God's children made in His image, and He loves us so much more than the boundaries of human love. For any of us who have had a child who went a different way, we can start to understand God's love for us. Our every thought is toward our child. Our heart's desire is for that child to turn from their ways and turn back to God. We want them to live full, productive, and happy lives. We want nothing more for them than to have a close, intimate relationship with God. We feel as though we would sacrifice everything we have for them to be changed. How much more so with God? We are limited in what we can do for our child but not God. We don't understand what our child truly needs to change but not so with God. God knows exactly what each and every one of us needs. He doesn't cast us off forever, nor afflict us willingly to crush us all as He is definitely able to do (Lam 3:31–35). God casts us off and afflicts us to turn us back to Him. God turns from us for a little while. With a little wrath, God hides Himself from us for a moment, but with great mercies and everlasting kindness, God will gather us and have mercy on us (Rom 11:30–32; Isa 54:7–8).

That is God's ultimate purpose: all mankind is His family. When Jesus told us that He and the Father have been working until now, the work He was talking about was bringing all mankind back to Him. God will use all of His power to accomplish this. Thank God!

There's a chapter in the book about the city of Sodom. I use the example of Sodom because the city and people of Sodom give us a complete picture of God's love, grace, and overall plan to restore our relationship with Him. Sodom was a wicked place—so wicked that God totally destroyed Sodom, the surrounding cities, and the plains. It's this total destruction of Sodom that makes us know that any prophecies and promises regarding Sodom must be for the time of the second resurrection—the resurrection of the unjust. Scripture reveals to us that the people of Sodom will not be thrown into hell, to burn for an eternity as we've all been taught. Rather, God tells us that the people of Sodom will be part of His family. God is restoring His relationship with the people of Sodom and will use that same plan to bring all mankind back to Him. My hope in writing this book is to show—using God's word found in the Holy Bible—that He does have a plan for all mankind and that plan is for each and every one of us to be His children and live eternally with Him.

THE RESURRECTIONS

AN OLD TESTAMENT VIEW

In the book of Acts, there's a passage where Paul was taken into custody by the Romans to protect him from the Jewish leadership who wanted to kill him for preaching Jesus Christ. The commander of the garrison, wanting to know what truly happened, took Paul before the Sanhedrin (the Jewish leadership) and allowed both sides to give their story. There was a point in Paul's defense of himself that he realized that the room was filled with Pharisees and Sadducees (two sects within the Jewish leadership). Paul knew they were divided over the resurrection of the dead. The Sadducees believed there was no resurrection, and the Pharisees believed in the resurrection. Paul then cried out that he was a Pharisee and was being judged because of his hope in the resurrection of the dead. This caused a great dissension amongst them and ultimately became the first in a series of events that lead Paul to Rome (Acts 23:6–10).

At the time of Christ, there was division amongst the Jews regarding the idea that God would raise the dead. Although followers of Jesus Christ today believe in the resurrection of the dead, this is our starting point in laying a foundation for understanding God's plan to restore His relationship with all mankind. The Jewish leadership at the time of Christ was confused about the resurrection, but what did God's word tell them?

There are many scriptures in the Old Testament that give a clear understanding that there is a resurrection from the dead. In the book of 1 Samuel, we learn that God brings us to the grave, but He also brings us up from the grave (1 Sam 2:6). In the book of Job, we see anticipation for the time when our change comes after death (Job 14:14). There's also a clear reference to a physical resurrection in Job, when he looks forward to the time when he will see God in his flesh after he has died and is raised (Job 19:25–27). King David in the book of Psalms tells us he will be satisfied when he awakes to God's likeness and that all those who have died will bow before God (Ps 17:15; 22:29). In the book of Isaiah, we learn that God will swallow up death forever and wipe away all tears (Isa 25:8).

Some of the strongest references to the resurrection in the Old Testament come from Isaiah and Daniel. Isaiah tells us that God's dead shall live; that Isaiah along with the rest of those who died will arise from the dead (Isa 26:19). In the book of Daniel, he tells us that some of the dead will awake to everlasting life and some will awake to everlasting contempt (Dan 12:2–3).

You can see that even though there was disagreement between the Jewish leadership at the time of Christ regarding the resurrection, Scripture is very clear that there is a resurrection from the dead. These are only a few of the Scriptures that point to God resurrecting mankind at some future point in time.

JESUS THE FIRSTBORN OR FIRSTFRUIT

On the day of Pentecost (a Jewish feast day), when the Holy Spirit was first given to followers of Jesus Christ, all those filled with the Holy Spirit spoke in different languages giving a clear outward sign that the Holy Spirit was given as promised. This confused the crowd who stood by and heard them speaking in each one's native language. Peter stood before the crowds and explained what had happened. He told the crowd that their patriarch, David, was dead and buried and that his tomb was still with them. While David was alive, he prophesied that the Anointed One would rise from the dead. Peter goes on to say that the Anointed One was crucified by them, and God raised Him from the dead, and He now sits at the right hand of God (Acts 2:29–36). Up until that point, no one had risen from the dead. Jesus Christ was the first to be raised from the dead by God. He was the firstfruit of those who had died (1 Cor 15:20).

For this discussion, it's enough to say that Israel would have been very comfortable with the concept of firstfruits because, God, in giving Israel the sacrificial system while they wandered in the desert, ordained that Israel bring the first (firstfruits) of all their produce to God as an offering (Lev 2:12). The people of Israel would bring the first produce of each harvest to the priests to thank God for blessing them. Israel was also instructed by God to give the firstborn of all livestock to Him for similar reasons. Early on, the firstborn male child was set apart for service to God and given the responsibility of supporting the high priest in his responsibilities. This responsibility was soon transferred to the tribe of Levi.

Scripture tells us that Jesus is the firstfruit of those who have fallen asleep (1 Cor 15:20). He is the firstborn over all creation; the firstborn into the world (Col 1:15–18; Heb 1:6). Jesus was and is the first to be risen from the dead (Acts 26:22–23; Rev 1:4–6). Through Adam, came death. Likewise, through Jesus Christ also came the resurrection of the dead. For as in Adam all die, even so in Jesus Christ all shall be made alive (1 Cor 15:21–32).

Jesus Christ's resurrection is basic to His followers, yet it was disputed by some in the early church (1 Cor 15:12). We need to be firmly rooted in this foundational belief for two reasons. First, Jesus's resurrection from the dead is the only sign that Jesus gave the religious leaders of His day to prove that He was the Anointed One (Matt 16:4). As Jonah was three days and three nights in the belly of a fish, so the Son of Man would be three days and three nights in the grave (Matt 12:40). The resurrection declares with power that Jesus is the Anointed One (Rom 1:1–4).

Second, if Jesus did not rise from the dead, then everything we hold onto is empty; our faith is also empty (1 Cor 15:13–19). If Jesus Christ did not rise, then all who have died have perished. Our assurance and living hope of the resurrection is through Jesus Christ's resurrection from the dead (Acts 17:30–31; 1 Peter 1:3–5, 20–21). God has given us this assurance by raising Jesus from the dead (John 14:19; Rom 5:10, 8:34–35; 1 Peter 3:18).

Jesus died once for all. Death no longer has dominion over Him (Rom 6:8–10). His death repaired our relationship with God. He is alive and dies no more. He lives that now having repaired our relationship with God, we may also live (2 Cor 5:14–15; Col 2:11–15).

Scripture tells us that God is not the God of the dead but of the living (Matt 22:31–32; Mark 12:27; Luke 20:38). The exceeding greatness of God's power raised Jesus from the dead (Eph 1:19–21; Acts 2:22–24, 5:30–32, 13:30–33; Rom 6:4). That same power will raise each of us from the dead (1 Cor 6:14; 2 Cor 4:14, 13:4; Rom 4:23–25; Gal 1:1; Phil 3:10–

11; 1 Thess 1:9–10; Heb 13:20–21). We have this assurance and can know God's power because Jesus Christ is risen and sits at the right hand of God continually interceding for us (Rom 8:34). It's the power of God's Holy Spirit living within us that gives life to our mortal bodies (Rom 8:11).

A NEW TESTAMENT VIEW

The apostles made sure that when miracles were performed, everyone knew that it was not their power that performed the miracle but by the power of Jesus Christ who was raised from the dead by the power of God (Acts 4:9–10). Paul customarily went to the synagogue on the Sabbath, explaining and demonstrating that Jesus is the Anointed One through His resurrection (Acts 17:2–3). They were all witnesses to His resurrection (Acts 1:21–22, 2:30–33, 3:14–16, 4:33). God showed Jesus openly yet chose specific individuals to witness Jesus's resurrection (Acts 10:40). The Bible tells us that Jesus revealed Himself to Peter, to the other apostles, to over five hundred of the brethren, to James, and finally to Paul—someone who had previously been persecuting those who followed Jesus (1 Cor 15:3–8). They ate and drank with Him after His resurrection (Acts 10:41–43). It's important to realize that even though they were all witnesses to the resurrection, they still needed the power of the Holy Spirit to proclaim Jesus as the Anointed One and His resurrection because persecution for that message was everywhere (Acts

4:1–2; 26:7–8, 26–27; 2 Tim 2:8–9). We'll talk more about the persecution of Jesus's followers later.

TWO RESURRECTIONS

As we saw earlier from the book of Daniel, Israel knew from the Scriptures that there were two groups of people that were going to be resurrected—some to everlasting life and some to shame and everlasting contempt (Dan 12:2). The resurrection of the dead was an elementary principle in the early church as well, but the writers of the New Testament were given much more insight from God on the resurrection (Heb 6:1–2). In the New Testament, we learn that there are actually two separate resurrections: those who have done good to the resurrection of life and those who have done evil to the resurrection of condemnation (Matt 25:46; John 5:28–29; Acts 24:15). They elsewhere are referred to as the resurrection of the just and the unjust. We also know that these two resurrections will occur at different times. The first resurrection is the resurrection of the just. They will be resurrected at Jesus's second coming. The second resurrection, the resurrection of the unjust will occur one thousand years later (Rev 20:4–5). We will now look at each resurrection a little more closely.

Jesus told His followers that those who did something for someone and weren't looking for a reward would be blessed and repaid at the resurrection of the just (Luke 14:14). He also said that all those who belong to Him will be raised up at the last day and have everlasting life and that even though they will die physically, they would pass from death to life (John 6:39–40, 44, 54, 11:25–26). After dying, they will hear Jesus's voice and live (John 5:24–27). The last day here refers to Jesus Christ's second coming. At His second coming, Jesus will set up His kingdom here on earth (Matt 25:31–34). At that time, all God's people and His prophets who had previously died will be resurrected into His kingdom (Matt 19:28; Luke 22:29). With a shout, with the voice of an archangel, and with a great sound of a trumpet, Jesus will gather all His elect from the four winds, from one end of heaven to the other (Matt 24:31). God's people and prophets who have died will rise first. They will be given incorruptible, immortal bodies. Then in a moment, in the twinkling of an eye, those of God's people who are alive at Jesus's second coming will be changed from the corruptible, mortal bodies they now have to incorruptible, immortal bodies. All God's people, those who previously died and those changed at Jesus's second coming will be caught up together in the clouds and meet Jesus and His angels in the air (1 Cor 15:51–53; 1 Thess 4:13–18). Again, this is referred to in the Bible as the first resurrection. Anyone resurrected or changed at the first resurrection have eternal life so death no longer reigns over them.

These resurrected people will have positions or responsibilities of kings, priests, and princes in the kingdom of God. They will be given authority over all God's physical creation under

Jesus Christ our king. All peoples and nations will be ruled and judged by God's people. God's kingdom, with Jesus Christ as King, and all God's people ruling under Him will reign over mankind for one thousand years (Rev 20:4–6). Satan will be bound during this time so mankind living during this one thousand year period will experience life with God ruling and not have the influence of Satan in the world (Rev 20:1–2).

After the one-thousand-year reign of God's kingdom, the resurrection of all those people who have ever lived but did not have a relationship with God will take place. As stated previously, this resurrection is known as the second resurrection, or Great White Throne judgment (the description of God's throne). The grave and the sea will give up their dead, those small and great, and they will be judged according to their works. Anyone found written in the book of life will have eternal life and anyone not found written in the book of life will be thrown into the lake of fire (this is known as the second death) (Rev 20:11–14).

Traditionally, we view the second resurrection as a single event. God raises the dead, they're judged, and then condemned. However, the text does not confine us to a specific period of time. In other words, there can be a period of time assigned by God for the judgment. It's clear that God raises the dead and they are judged, but the length of that judgment period is not specified anywhere in the Bible. We will see in the judgment chapters how God will use this judgment period.

Another point we typically overlook regarding the second resurrection is that there are those who have eternal life as a result of their judgment, yet these people were not raised in the first resurrection—the resurrection of God's people. It could be said that these people are people who lived during the one-thousand-year reign of Jesus. These people may make up in part the people raised in the second resurrection who are written in the book of life, but again, the text does not limit eternal life to be given to those people only. As our study progresses, we'll see who these additional people are that have eternal life as a result of the judgment. A change happens during this judgment period that turns these lost people to God.

It's interesting to note that Satan will be released after the thousand-year-reign of Jesus and His people. He will go out and deceive the inhabitants of the earth, and they will actually revolt against God (Rev 20:1–3). It's not known for sure whether or not Satan will be allowed to influence those resurrected in the second resurrection, but the timing aligns for Satan's release and the second resurrection. We'll see how this plays into God's plan later. It makes sense that this would happen, that God would resurrect these people, give them new conditions to live their lives, and allow Satan to influence them as he has us now. However, the Scriptures are not perfectly clear on this.

At this point I think it's important to make a few points about the resurrection from the dead. I have to wonder how real the resurrection really is to us who are followers of Jesus. We know from Scripture that our hope for the future is absolutely tied to the resurrection of Jesus from the dead. God showed His great power in raising Jesus from the dead. That same power will raise each and every human being when God decides that it's time.

However, we seldom talk of the resurrection in our sermons, Bible studies, or general conversation. Any talk of a future life centers around going to heaven. This concept has dominated our teaching. We think of the time when we die as an immediate release into a spiritual life. We will be with God, see Him face-to-face, and be rejoined with family and friends who have gone before us. These are nice thoughts that give us comfort, especially as we experience death in our lives or approach death ourselves. This idea is fine and has some Biblical support. However, we need to always keep God's word and promises to us in the front of our minds. The problem I see is that the truth of God's word is masked by this traditional thinking. It's almost as if the resurrection is unreal or not important to us. Who cares if we are resurrected when we're already in heaven? Why would we be interested in life back here on earth when we're with God in His home (wherever that is)?

God clearly tells us in His word that we will be raised from the dead and live again with the earth as our home. Those who are members of His family will have bodies like

Jesus had after He was raised from the dead (1 Cor 15:42, 49; Phil 3:21). We will have bodies that can be seen, touched, and we will be able to converse with others (Matt 28:9; Mark 16:12; John 20:27). Yet we will also be spirit; transcending time and physical boundaries (John 20:19, 26). Those who are raised in the second resurrection will have physical bodies as they do today, and they will be placed in their lands as before death (Ezek 37:1–14). This is our hope and guarantee from God.

SODOM

THE ANCIENT CITY

Sodom was an ancient city that was thriving during the time of Abraham (the patriarch of Israel). It was located in the plains of Jordan, bordering the territory of Canaan. The plains of Jordan were well-watered everywhere like the land of Egypt and the garden of the Lord. It was a desirable place to live, so when Abraham and his nephew, Lot, decided to separate their livestock and settle in different areas, Lot chose the valley of Jordan because of its beauty and fertile land. Lot and his family traveled east toward Sodom, and Abraham and his family settled in Canaan. That's when we first learn of Sodom's wickedness in the eyes of the Lord (Gen 10:19, 13:10–13).

Not much else is known about Sodom. The king of Sodom joined forces with four other kings to battle against Chedorlaomer king of Elam and three other kings. During this war, Lot was taken hostage along with his family, livestock, and all his goods. When Abraham found out, he took three hundred eighteen trained servants, divided them by night, and attacked. Abraham was able to bring back Lot and his family and all their goods (Gen 14:8–16).

The Bible describes the wickedness of Sodom in great detail. They were an exceedingly wicked and sinful people (Gen 13:13). They gave themselves over to adultery, immorality, perverse acts of homosexuality, rape, and giving themselves over to strange flesh (Jude 7, Gen 19:4–5). They walked in lies and strengthened the hand of evildoers so that no one turned back from their wickedness (Jer 23:14). They were full of food and abundant in idleness, yet they didn't lift a hand to help the needy (Ezek 16:49–50). They were so prideful that they declared their sins and didn't try to hide them (Isa 3:9). The outcry against Sodom was so great and their sins so grave that it was heard by God (Gen 18:20–21). Sounds like our society today, doesn't it?

The Bible uses the word *sodomite* (people of Sodom) to describe ritual harlots and perverted people (1 Cor 6:9–11; 1 Tim 1:8–11). The word became synonymous with any sexual activity that was perverse in nature. The word *sodomy* is used to this day to describe perverse sexual intercourse.

God told Abraham that the outcry against Sodom and Gomorrah (a neighboring city) was great, and their sin was very grave, so it was His intention to go down and see their wickedness for Himself. Knowing Lot lived there, Abraham tried to intercede for Sodom. He asked God a series of questions, desiring to know if He would destroy the city if there were any righteous people living there. God concludes the conversation by letting Abraham know that He would not destroy the city if He found ten righteous people living there (Gen 18:20–21, 23–33). God saw Abraham's heart and knew that Lot's family was the only righteous family living in Sodom.

God sent two messengers to Sodom to get Lot and his family out so that God could destroy the city, the surrounding cities, and the plains where Sodom was located. The men of the city both old and young men from every quarter surrounded Lot's house and demanded that they be allowed essentially to rape the messengers. The men were stricken with blindness so that Lot and his family were protected. Lot was told to gather up his entire family so they could flee in the morning. His two son-in-law's thought he was joking and decided to stay behind (Gen 19:1, 10–14).

The next morning, Lot, his wife, and his two daughters left Sodom with the messengers from God (Gen 19:15–17). As soon as Lot and his family fled the city, God rained down brimstone (a flammable material similar to sulfur) and fire upon the cities and plains, destroying all people and vegetation. The smoke from the destruction went up like the smoke of a furnace and was seen from miles away by Abraham (Gen 19:23–28). The destruction was complete and happened in a moment's time (Lam 4:6). As a result, the whole land was brimstone, salt, and burning; it was not sown nor did it bear any crops nor did grass grow there (Deut 29:23). Sodom and the surrounding cities ceased to exist. God's judgment was final. No one would remain there nor would any human dwell there (Isa 13:19–20; Jer 49:18, 50:40; Amos 4:11). That's exactly what happened. No one has ever lived in that area since its destruction. It is overrun with weeds and salt pits, and is in a state of perpetual desolation (Zeph 2:9).

On the day that God rained fire and brimstone on the people of Sodom and Gomorrah, they were going about their everyday life, eating and drinking, buying and selling, and planting and building. God uses their example to show what will also happen to the world at the second coming of Jesus Christ (Luke 17:28–30; Rom 9:29).

God condemned Sodom to destruction, making it an example to those who afterward would live ungodly. They were set forth as an example, suffering the vengeance of eternal fire (Jude 5–7, 2 Peter 2:6). Pretty heavy stuff! Sodom and the surrounding cities were destroyed and haven't been inhabited in approximately four thousand years now. Today, some archaeologists believe they've found the site where Sodom was located. Regardless of whether or not that's true, we can definitely say that Sodom as a city and as a people are gone. God completely destroyed the city—all its inhabitants and all vegetation as an example to us of what will happen to those who do not turn from wickedness. But that's not the end of the story.

JERUSALEM'S SISTER

In a prophecy about Jerusalem (representing God's people Israel), God causes Ezekiel to compare Jerusalem to Samaria and Sodom. Samaria was very similar to Sodom in its corruption and wickedness, but Samaria was not destroyed by God like Sodom was. Ezekiel refers to Samaria as Jerusalem's elder sister, and Sodom as Jerusalem's younger sister. Through Ezekiel, God tells us that if it weren't enough that Jerusalem's sisters were disgusting and loathsome to God, Jerusalem became even more corrupt than her sisters. God tells us that neither Samaria nor Sodom did what Jerusalem did (Ezek 16:46–48). Can you imagine that? Israel was even more corrupt than Sodom was—the city that God completely destroyed. God then reminds Jerusalem of why He punished Sodom. Sodom was prideful. They were blessed with abundance so much so that they became lazy and didn't care for those in need. They were haughty and committed disgusting acts before God, so God destroyed them (Ezek 16:49–50). Jerusalem was actually more corrupt than Sodom.

God tells Jerusalem that her sins were twice what her sister Samaria's sins were. Therefore, because of Jerusalem's wicked ways, Samaria and Sodom were made acceptable before God. God tells Jerusalem she judged her sisters, yet her sins were more than theirs. Therefore, they are more righteous than Jerusalem. Be disgraced and ashamed, Jerusalem, because your wickedness makes your sisters acceptable before God (Ezek 16:51–52). Samaria and Sodom are acceptable before God? They are more righteous than Jerusalem? What does this mean, especially for Sodom, the city that was completely destroyed some fourteen hundred years before? How are they made acceptable? When are they made acceptable?

This is where the prophecy gets really interesting! God says that when He brings back the people of Samaria and Sodom, He'll bring back the people of Israel. Then Jerusalem will be ashamed by how she comforted her sisters. When God returns Samaria and Sodom to their former states, then God will return Jerusalem to her former state (Ezek 16:53–59). Remember, Sodom was completely destroyed around fourteen hundred years earlier and had not been inhabited up to Ezekiel's time and hasn't been inhabited since. To this day, the city of Sodom is no more. So when God tells us that He is going to restore Sodom to its former state, He's referring to the second resurrection. These were all wicked people in God's sight. The Israelites, the people of Samaria, and the people of Sodom were wicked and died that way. They were all corrupt, disgusting, and loathsome to God. So when God refers to Sodom, a wicked city that was destroyed some fourteen hundred years earlier and says He's going to bring them back to their former state, He's telling us about the second resurrection, the resurrection of judgment for the wicked, also known as the Great White Throne judgment. We see then a picture of God resurrecting the dead and bringing them back to their former state. It's then and only then that they realize their error and are ashamed and disgraced by their behavior (Ezek 16:61).

At this point, we leave this prophecy and turn to a vision God gave to Ezekiel. We'll come back to this prophecy because God has much more to say about Sodom's future.

THE VALLEY OF DRY BONES

In a vision, God took Ezekiel to a valley that's full of bones. There were many bones filling the valley, and they were very dry. The fact that there were many bones filling the valley tells us that they represented a large number of people who had previously died. The bones being very dry tells us these bones had been there for many, many years; that the people had been dead for many, many years (Ezek 37:1–2).

God asked Ezekiel if these bones could live, to which Ezekiel humbly responded that only God could know that. God told Ezekiel to prophecy to the bones and tell them that God would cover them with tissue and flesh and put breath into them so they would live. It's at this point, when God brings these bones back to life; that the people know that God is Lord, when He puts breath in them, and they live (Ezek 37:3–6). The strong implication here is that prior to

God resurrecting these people, they did not know God nor have a relationship with Him. In their prior life, they were separated from God.

God also told Ezekiel that these people are the whole house of Israel (Ezek 37:11). We know that all but a remnant of Israel rejected God completely. This then, along with the fact that these people didn't know God prior to being resurrected tells us that this resurrection is not the first resurrection—the resurrection of God's people at Jesus Christ's second coming—but pictures the second resurrection as we saw in the previous prophecy about Jerusalem, Samaria, and Sodom. This is where our two stories connect. Both the prophecy of Jerusalem, Samaria and Sodom, and the vision of the valley of dry bones are picturing the second resurrection—the resurrection of judgment. In both cases, there is a resurrection of the dead, and the people being resurrected have not had a relationship with God to that point. In both cases, the people being resurrected recognize the error of their ways after being given life again.

Continuing on with Ezekiel's vision, Ezekiel then prophesied to the bones as he was told and witnessed the bones rattling and coming together and tissue and flesh coming upon them. However, they were still not living, so God told Ezekiel to prophecy to the breath and tell the breath to come from the four winds and breathe on these dead people so that they may live. Ezekiel prophesied as he was commanded. Breath came into the bone, and they lived (Ezek 37:7–10).

Ezekiel witnessed this large army of people coming to life before him. What an amazing sight that must have been. A whole valley filled with dry bones are reconstructed into human beings and brought back to life by God. As mentioned earlier, God tells Ezekiel that this army represents the whole house of Israel. There are many scriptures in the New Testament that clearly state that God's people, Israel, are not children of the flesh, but His children through the promise (Rom 9:6–8; Gal 4:21–26, 6:15–16; Heb 12:22–24). What that's telling us is that physical Israel was a type for God's spiritual family. God's family is made up of all mankind who turn to Him and repent. Therefore, when God gives us a picture of the whole house of Israel being resurrected, He's giving us a picture of all people from the beginning of time that rejected or didn't know Him at the second resurrection. They are all brought back to life. It's at this point that they recognize that they've been cut off from God. Their previous lives were lived apart from God. They followed their own desires and rejected God, and they rejected Jesus Christ (or didn't know Him). Therefore, they realize now as they're brought back to life that their behavior cut them off from God. How hopeless and lost they feel. Do you see the connection with the other prophecy where Jerusalem is disgraced and ashamed?

Think of all the people who ever lived that are cut off from God. People who lived wicked, sinful lives; people who were good citizens yet had no room for God; people who knew God but the cares of the world choked off any true connection with God; people who didn't even know of God, whether from an early death or living in a region where God could only be known of through His creation—all these people were being brought back to life and were realizing at that point that they are hopeless because God was never a part of their lives.

God opens their graves, brings them back to life, and puts them back in their lands (Ezek 37:12–13). They aren't raised, judged immediately, and then punished eternally. As a matter of fact, the opposite happens. God raises them and puts them in their lands. At this point, they know that God is Lord, when He brings them to life and puts them in their land. Sometime during the process of raising mankind from the dead and having them live in their own lands they come to know God and desire a relationship with Him. When you look at what has just happened to these people, it's more than just an "ah-ha" moment. They've experienced their own death (and whatever pain led up to that), they're now resurrected to life; they come face-to-face with God and then are put back into their lands. I'd say this experience will rock even the most rebellious of us. God then puts His Spirit in these resurrected people and they live—live eternally (Ezek 37:14).

SODOM'S INHERITANCE

Now, back to the prophecy Ezekiel was given regarding Jerusalem, Samaria, and Sodom. God told Israel that regardless of their wickedness and rejection of Him, He would remember His covenant with Israel and establish an everlasting covenant with them (Ezek 16:60). In a profound way, God demonstrates His grace toward mankind by forgiving all the sins of the past and establishing an everlasting covenant with mankind (just like God's grace has been poured out on God's people today). We need to realize that just because God may have called you to Himself in this lifetime and poured out His grace on you that God's grace should not or cannot be poured out on all mankind at the second resurrection. It is God who decides who and when He will draw to Himself. Nowhere does the Bible state that our relationship with God can only be repaired here and now, and if we die before God calls us to Himself, we're lost. We make those constraints, not God.

When God has done all these things for Israel, they will be ashamed. God will give Samaria and Sodom to Jerusalem as daughters, and Israel will receive them (Ezek 16:61–63). Realize what this is saying. God is making an everlasting covenant with all mankind. We've already seen how wicked and corrupt Sodom was and how God destroyed the city and people of Sodom as an example for all of us. Now God is saying that He is making an everlasting covenant with Israel, and he is giving the people of Sodom to Israel as daughters. God is extending His everlasting covenant to Sodom, Samaria, and all mankind. God then says that He will provide atonement for Jerusalem (Israel, Samaria, Sodom, and mankind). That atonement is Jesus Christ (Rom 5:9-11; Isa 25:7–9).

THE JUDGMENT

JUDGMENT OF ALL

God tells us that it's been appointed for all men to die once, and it's also appointed for all men to be judged (Heb 9:27–28). We may not realize it, but God judges both the just and the unjust (Acts 24:15). For those that belong to God, judgment is in this current life (1 Pet 4:17). Those who overcome shall not be hurt by the second death (discussed in the Resurrections chapter) (Rev 2:11). For those who have rejected God, judgment comes later in the second resurrection as we saw previously (Rev 11:18; 14:7). Most often in our study of the Scriptures, judgment is viewed in a very negative way. However, if God's followers are being judged today, we can get a framework of God's perspective on judgment by looking at how His people will be judged.

God clearly warns mankind that unless we repent, we will all perish (Luke 13:2–5). As stated in the introduction, there's no questioning the elementary principle of eternal judgment

(Heb 6:1–2). God states over and over again that if we do not repent of our sins and if we do not believe that Jesus is the Anointed One, we will die in our sins (John 8:21, 24). God is righteous, and His judgments are true and righteous (Rev 16:5–7). When God's kingdom is firmly established here on earth, all nations will know God's righteous judgments because they will be manifested before them (Rev 15:4). God's purpose in His judgment is to turn all mankind to Him. God will seek out the wickedness in each of us until He finds none (Ps 10:15). He afflicts us until we change but then afflicts us no more (Nah 1:12). He gives understanding to those that have erred, and those that have complained will learn doctrine (Isa 29:22–24). Those that God calls to Himself are broken, and those that reject God are ground to powder (Luke 20:18). The point is that God works in each one of our lives in His timing, and all are refined by fire (Mark 9:49).

God tells us He has no pleasure in the death of the wicked. His desire is that all the wicked turn from their evil ways. He states over and over again that if the wicked turns from their wickedness, they shall live. All sins are forgotten when the wicked turn away from sin (Ezek 18:21–23, 27–32, 33:11, 14–20).

Speaking from my own experience, I can look back and see how God was working with me from a young age. I would look at the Bible displayed in our living room, and the thought would come to me that God's truth was somewhere hidden within its pages. I would try to read but wasn't ready or willing to give myself over to God. As a young adult, I did many, many very stupid and dangerous things I'm not proud of. Looking back, I can see how God protected me from my stupidity and directed me, yet I still refused to turn to Him. Finally, in college, I got to a point where I had totally messed up everything. I wasn't working. I had a huge student loan debt. I was kicked out of school for failing every class, and I was partying heavily. It was at that point that I broke down and asked God to forgive me and pleaded with Him to take over my life because I couldn't continue on that way. In a quiet, calm voice, God told me to start working. The next morning, I found a job opening in the paper. I was interviewed that day, and started working the next day. That was the changing point in my life. Thankfully, God never gave up on me! It wasn't me that brought about the changes in my life; it was God and God alone!

God tells us He will swallow up death forever, wipe away tears from all faces, and take away the rebuke of His people (Isa 25:7–9). He will return us to the days of our youth, causing us to pray to Him. God will delight in us so we shall see His face with joy; for He will restore to us His righteousness and redeem us from the grave so our life shall see light (Job 33:23–28). These are amazing statements. God will show mercy and restore our relationship with Him. This will only happen after we have a change of heart; after we return to God.

First of all, we need to be clear that just because people lived and died without having a relationship with God for whatever reason—whether they were born before Jesus Christ walked the earth or their cultures were too different to accept Christ or they lived in an area where the good news about the kingdom of God had never been preached, God revealed Himself to us all through His creation. If you stop and ponder any of the miracles of creation, their complexity, their beauty, and their complete harmony (not to mention life itself), then you will realize that they can only be explained by an almighty all powerful loving Creator God at their origin. Therefore, no one can make the excuse that they didn't know God or that God has never revealed Himself to them. God tells us that we know of Him yet refuse to glorify Him or thank Him for everything He gives us (Rom 1:20–25). Mankind, in our vanity and pride, rejected God and refused to submit to Him, so God gave us over to the lusts of our hearts. We've exchanged the truth God has revealed to us in creation for the lie that God doesn't exist, so we end up making idols for ourselves and worship the idol instead of God.

The perfect example of our rejection of God is the teaching on evolution. When Darwin developed his ideas about evolution, he knew there was no fossil evidence to support them. He assumed that some day as science advanced, the evidence would be revealed. To this day, there is no scientific proof of evolution and yet that's what's taught in our schools as truth. The clear evidence of a Creator God as witnessed in creation is rejected for a theory developed by man that has no foundation.

God through creation, reveals Himself to all mankind in this life, and God also reveals Himself to all mankind after this life while we are still in the grave. There's a controversial passage in 1 Peter that tells us that God preaches the good news of His kingdom to those who never knew Him prior to their resurrection to judgment so that they may be judged according to the flesh and the lives they previously lived, but more importantly so that they may also live eternally (1 Peter 4:3–6). I've read many commentaries that try to explain away what Peter is clearly telling us because we don't fully understand God's plan for all mankind. However, once we open ourselves up to God's plan, the passage makes perfect sense just as it's written. God makes Himself known to man through creation and then reveals Himself to man while in the grave.

It is God who judges mankind, and He has given all authority over to Jesus Christ. God has committed all judgment to Christ and ordained Him to judge the living and the dead (John 5:22–23; Acts 10:40–42; 1 Cor 4:4; 5:12–13; 2 Tim 4:1). All mankind must appear before His judgment seat. Each will be judged according to what they have done in this life, whether good or bad (2 Cor 5:9–10). There is no creature hidden from His sight, but all things are naked and open to the eyes of Him to whom we must give account (Heb 4:13). Jesus tells us that for every idle word we speak we will give an account of it on the day of judgment (Matt 12:36).

GOD JUDGES OUR WORKS

God desires mercy and not sacrifice (Matt 9:13, 12:7; 1 Peter 2:9–10). He wants us to show love and compassion on each other, and not to do things because we're commanded to, but because it's our hearts desire. All of us receive mercy from God, so God expects us to do the same for others; to show each other mercy (Luke 10:36–37). In the day of our judgment, God will give us the same measure of mercy we give to others (James 2:12–13). He tells us to not judge, and we shall not be judged; to condemn not, and we shall not be condemned; to forgive, and we will be forgiven (Luke 6:37–38). God judges us without partiality, according to our works (1 Peter 1:17). Everyone who exalts themselves will be humbled, and everyone who humbles themselves will be exalted (Luke 18:13–14). If our forgiveness of our brother's trespasses is not from our heart, then God will not forgive us (Matt 18:33–35). We need to realize that God's ultimate purpose is not judgment; it's mercy. God's mercy will ultimately triumph over judgment (James 2:13). In other words, God's mercy will prevail.

Jesus told us that whoever has, to him more will be given, and whoever does not have even what he seems to have will be taken away from him (Luke 8:16–18, 19:26–27). This saying may not make sense from a physical perspective or seem too harsh. Why would God give more to someone who already has? And for the person who has little, why would God take that away? We need to keep in mind that God is teaching us that everything we have, our physical life, circumstances, talents, and our spiritual understanding are from Him, so when He gives us something and we are prideful in our consideration of it, He will take it away from us and give it to someone who recognizes that everything they have is a blessing from Him. By doing so, the one who receives the gift glorifies God, and the one who had everything taken away will come to glorify God when their eyes are opened to Him. Again, God's ultimate purpose is to turn all mankind back to Him.

Some people's sins are clearly evident, preceding them to judgment, but the recognition of the sins of some follows later. Likewise, the good works of some are clearly evident, and those whose works are bad cannot hide them (1 Tim 5:24–25). We cannot hide our actions or thoughts from God. He knows us better than we know ourselves. God sees all of our works and tests them with fire so that those whose works are burned will suffer loss but will be saved (1 Cor 3:15). Again, God's ultimate purpose is to turn all mankind back to Himself.

JUDGMENT OF THE JUST

THE COMMANDMENT OF JESUS CHRIST

A Jewish lawyer, wanting to test Jesus asked Him which is the great commandment in the law. Jesus replied that the first and great commandment was to love the Lord your God with all your heart, with all your soul, and with all your mind. He then went on to add that the second great command was to love your neighbor as yourself. On these two commandments hang all the law and the prophets (Matt 22:34–40; Mark 12:28–31). There is no other commandment greater than these. The apostle John helped clarify these two commandments for us. He tells us that we love God by believing in the name of Jesus Christ; believing that Jesus is God (1 John 3:22–23; 2 John 5). He also tells us that we cannot love God if we don't love our brother. If we don't love someone whom we can see, how can we love God whom we cannot see (1 John 4:20)?

We are to love from a pure heart, a good conscience, and a sincere faith (1 Tim 1:5; 2 Pet 1:5–7). Faith and brotherly love go hand in hand. We are to stand fast in the faith and let all that we do be done in love (1 Cor 16:13–14). We know we are God's children when we keep these commandments. They are not burdensome (1 John 5:1–3). God's love is perfected in us so that we may have boldness in the day of judgment (1 John 4:17–19). Our faith in Jesus Christ is our victory that overcomes the world (1 John 5:4–5). How wonderful it would be for us to be remembered for our unceasing work of faith and labor of love as Paul remembered the church in Thessalonica (1 Thess 1:3–4; 2 Thess 1:11–12). Let's now look at God's commandments to believe in Jesus Christ and to have brotherly love and see how God is judging His people today.

JUDGMENT OF THE JUST: FAITH

Following the law as given to Israel through Moses does not free us from blame before God. We are found blameless by faith in Jesus Christ (Phil 3:9). We become right with God through faith in Jesus Christ. He revealed the righteousness of God apart from the law (Rom 1:17). Before faith came, God's people were protected by the law and kept for the faith which would later be revealed through Jesus Christ. The law was a tutor to bring them to Christ so they could be found blameless by faith in Him (Gal 3:23–25; Rom 3:21–22). Now that faith is here, we are no longer under the law. In the book of Hebrews, we are given examples of living faith in those who walked before us and didn't receive the promise of Jesus Christ and the Holy Spirit (Heb 11). They all died not having received the promises, but having seen them from afar were assured of them. All those before us are being made perfect with us through faith (Heb 11:13, 39–40).

We are told to live by faith, for without faith it's impossible to please God. Those who come to God must believe that He is God, and that He rewards those who diligently seeking Him (Hab 2:4; Heb 11:6). So then we need to understand God's definition of faith. Faith is being sure of things we hope for and yet cannot see. By faith, we understand that the worlds were framed by the word of God so that the things which are seen are not made by things that are visible (Heb 11:1–3). Jesus told Thomas that those who haven't seen Him yet believe in him are blessed (John 20:29). By faith, we believe in God and Jesus Christ. We believe that God the Father and Jesus Christ are one. We also believe in the works that Jesus performed and know that they came from God. By faith, we believe that Jesus was sent from the Father and died and rose again (John 6:29, 40, 7:38-39, 10:37–38, 11:25, 12:44–46, 14:1, 10–11, 16:26–27, 17:8, 20:30–31; Eph 1:15–21; 1 Thess 4:14; James 2:19). We see then that for us, faith is knowing God and His plan for us by knowing that Jesus is God and believing in His words to us. We know these things not because we see them. We know these things because God has revealed them to us, and we believe.

By God's power and grace, we are saved through faith. Even our faith is a gift from God, so none of us can boast and say it was by our doing that we've been saved (Eph 2:8–9; Rom 3:27–31). God restores our relationship with Him by His power through faith (1 Peter 1:5). By faith in Jesus Christ, we are sons of God and have eternal life. We believe that since God raised Jesus from the dead He is able and will raise us from the dead (Luke 8:15; Mark 16:16; John 3:15–16, 5:24, 6:47, 11:25–26, 20:31; Acts 4:12, 16: 31, 13:39, 48; Gal 3:26).

Our actions, our behaviors, and our works are the results of the faith we have (James 2:26). We will know the strength of our faith by our works. We can do so much if we only have faith. Jesus tells us that if we have faith, we will do even greater works than He did (John 14:12–14). If we have even a small measure of faith, we can command changes on the earth, and they will be so (Matt 17:20; Mark 11:23; Luke 17:6). Nothing is impossible for us.

Our faith is much more precious to us than gold that perishes. Therefore, God tells us that the genuineness of our faith is tested by fire, so that at Jesus Christ's second coming, we will find praise, honor, and glory (1 Peter 1:7). God rebukes and chastens those He loves, so when we are faced with fiery trials, we should not think it's strange that these things are happening to us (Rev 3:19). Rather, we should rejoice to the extent that we are partakers of Christ's suffering

(1 Peter 4:12–13). To say it another way, our reaction to life's difficulties indicates how strong our faith really is. Jesus sends us a strong warning in the book of Luke. He poses the question: "When the Son of Man comes, will He really find faith on the earth?" (Luke 18:8). So then let's look at the many ways God is testing our faith in action.

FAITH IN ACTION

Scripture identifies the many ways our faith is tested. Keep in mind that the time has come for judgment to begin at the house of God. God is judging our faith; He is judging how we allow Him to live in our lives and lead our lives. In this section, I don't go deep into each topic since each topic could support a significant discussion that would take us outside the scope of this book. Rather, I pull out key verses from Scripture to show that each is driven by our faith.

Jesus tells us that all things are possible to those who believe (Mark 9:23). If we believe that we will receive what we ask for when we pray, we will have them (Mark 11:24; Matt 21:22). Ask and it will be given to you; seek and you will find; knock and it will be opened to you. Everyone who asks receives, those who seek find, and to those whom knock the door is opened. We are to believe that we will receive what we ask for and be persistent in asking (Matt 7:7–11; Luke 11:8–13).

There tends to be two approaches to prayer in the church. There are those who believe that we can do anything if we believe, and we are aligned with God's will. There are others who take these scriptures more literally. They believe that if our faith is strong enough, anything is possible for us to do; there's nothing that we cannot make happen. What I can say with certainty from my own life is that when my prayers are from the heart and my motives are not selfish God has always answered. In other words, I'm asking for what I desire, but my desires are aligned with God because I've submitted my life to Him. Where the problem comes is with our understanding of what faith is and what faith isn't. Faith is trusting in God for everything we have and all our needs, and doing His will. Faith isn't some supernatural power we have apart from God. So then I think both approaches are correct as long as we keep our eyes on God. When we say that our faith is strong, what we're actually saying is that we've given ourselves over to God and are aligned with Him and His word. Our thoughts are not based on our desires but on His. It's not our power at work but the Holy Spirit living within us. Amazing things can and will be done through the prayers of those who truly believe. Prayer is faith in action.

Jesus told us He came to send fire on earth. He didn't come to bring peace; He came to bring division. Homes will be divided: Father against son and son against father, mother against daughter and daughter against mother, and mother-in-law against her daughter-in-law and daughter-in-law against her mother-in-law (Luke 12:49–53). Jesus went as far as to say that anyone coming to Him to be His follower has to hate his father and mother, wife and children, brothers and sisters, yes, and his own life also. We must bear our cross and come after Him to be His followers (Luke 14:26–27, 33, 18:29–30). We can disagree on what He meant by hate, but the bottom line is many who follow Jesus Christ may be rejected by their families because they put God first in their lives. We must forsake all to be His follower. Jesus concludes His statements on division by promising blessings for anyone who has been rejected by their family because of Him (Mark 10:29–30). We become part of His family and are blessed with eternal life. Division and loss of loved ones caused by following Jesus Christ are faith in action.

As Jesus was journeying along a road, He was approached by people wanting to follow Him. One said he would follow Jesus wherever He went. Another responded to Jesus invitation to follow Him by asking to first go and bury his father. Another man said he would follow Jesus but first needed to bid farewell to his family. Jesus's response was to tell the men to let the dead bury their own. No one—having put their hand to the plow and looking back—is fit for the kingdom of God (Luke 9:57–62).

In another instance, a ruler who kept the law from his youth wanted to know what he needed to do to have eternal life. Jesus told him to sell all that he had and distribute it to the poor, and he would have treasure in heaven. Unfortunately, the man was very rich and couldn't leave his treasures behind, so he left very sorrowful. Jesus also became sorrowful and so He used the incident to teach His disciples. He told them it's easier for a camel to go through the eye of a needle than for a rich man to enter the kingdom of God (Luke 18:18–25).

The point in these passages is that if we are to be followers of Jesus Christ, it takes more than just saying we are. We will have to leave the riches and cares of this world behind and give our lives over to God. That doesn't mean we all become missionaries in third world countries. God has blessed some with that calling but not all of us. We are all blessed with spiritual gifts, and God will use each of us in unique ways to further His plan. Leaving the cares and riches of this world behind to follow Jesus is faith in action.

Satan wants to destroy us. He seeks to devour us. That's why Jesus told us when praying, ask God to deliver us from the evil one's temptations (Matt 6:13). We can never try to turn responsibility from ourselves. It's not God who is tempting us. When we're tempted it's us giving in to our desires (James 1:13–15). We are to be sober and vigilant in our faith; that it's our faith that strengthens us to resist the devil (1 Peter 5:8–9). Our flesh is weak and will give in to temptation, but God's Spirit in us will help us (Matt 26:41; Mark 14:38). All that tempts us is common to mankind, but since we belong to God, He is faithful and will deliver us from temptation. God will not allow us to be tempted beyond what we are able to resist. He will always provide a way to escape the temptation so that we can bear it (2 Peter 2:9; 1 Cor 10:13). Our part is believing that He will do what He promises and use the shield of our faith to quench all the fiery darts of the wicked one (Eph 6:16).

God also wants us to bear each other's burdens. We have all been overcome by temptation, so when we see a fellow servant of God who has been overtaken, we who are more spiritually mature should restore them with a spirit of gentleness (Gal 6:1–2).

We are blessed and approved when we endure temptation (James 1:12). It's not us imposing our will that overcomes temptation. Rather, we become more and more sickened by our behaviors as our faith grows, and we allow the Holy Spirit to guide our lives. God frees us from temptation when our hearts want the wall removed that's separating us from God, and we believe that it is only through His power that we will overcome. Overcoming temptation by giving it over to God is faith in action.

Israel's history is riddled with persecution of the prophets and God's people. The prophets were killed for foretelling of the coming of the Just One. They spoke in the name of the Lord and are an example to us of suffering and patience (Acts 7:52–53). James tells us the suffering of Job was revealed to us so we can understand that the Lord is very compassionate and merciful (James 5:9–11).

The church from its humble beginnings suffered persecution (Phil 1:29–30). We are reminded of the persecution of the prophets to encourage us (Matt 5:12). We suffer at the hands of our countrymen as they did and we are blessed as they were when persecution is for righteousness sake (1 Thess 2:14–16; Rom 5:1–5). Jesus tells us that persecution will be without basis. There will be all kinds of evil done against us for His sake (Matt 5:10–11).

We should not marvel that the world hates us (1 John 3:13). A student is not above his teacher nor is a servant above his master (Matt 10:24–26). Jesus suffered persecution unjustly, so we should expect the same. All who desire to live godly in Jesus Christ will suffer persecution (2 Tim 3:12). Jesus said if the world hates us; know that it hated Him before it hated us (John 15:18–21). His prayer for His followers was that God would not take them out of the world, but that He would keep them from the evil one (John 17:14–18). The followers of Jesus were hated because they were not of the world just as Jesus was not of the world.

Persecution builds our faith. Our persecution weakens us physically, but we are not destroyed (2 Cor 4:8–10). Rather through persecution, we become strong spiritually (2 Cor 12:10). God uses our persecution to strengthen our faith. He also uses persecution to accomplish His purposes in spreading the good news about His kingdom. The church may never have grown beyond Judea as it did if persecution hadn't driven the followers of Jesus from Jerusalem (Acts 8:4).

There are many types of persecution. People will hate us and exclude us. We will be thought of as evil (Luke 6:22–23). We will be brought before church councils, put in prison, and beaten (Matt 10:16–18; Mark 13:9–10). We will be betrayed by family and friends. Some of us will be put to death (Matt 10:21–23, 24:9–13; Luke 21:12–19). Those persecuting us will think they are doing God's service. Jesus tells us all these things to prepare us for what will happen (John 16:1–4). However, He also tells us not to worry about persecution or what we will say in defense of ourselves because the Holy Spirit is always with us and will give us everything we need at that time. It will not be us speaking but the Spirit of our Father who speaks in us (Matt 10:19–20; Mark 13:11–13).

God tells us that we are blessed when we suffer for doing good. When we are aligned with God's will and suffer, it's better than suffering for doing evil (1 Peter 3:14–17). If we endure our suffering to the end, we are saved. Our patience and faith in all the persecutions and severe troubles we endure are evidence of the righteous judgment of God so we may be counted worthy of His kingdom (2 Thess 1:3-5). If we are faithful to the end, God will give us a crown of righteousness (Rev 6:9–11, 2:10, 12:11). We have a sure promise from God that persecutions will not separate us from the love of Christ (Rom 8:35). We are His children and heirs of God and joint heirs with Christ (Rom 8:17). Enduring and overcoming persecutions are evidence of faith in action.

In the book of Matthew, there's an account where Jesus sent His disciples away in a boat while He dismissed a crowd and spent time alone in prayer. While at sea, the boat was tossed by the wind. Jesus came to the disciples by walking across the water. When Peter realized it was Jesus, he got out of the boat and started walking toward Jesus on the water. He quickly realized what he was doing and began to sink. He cried out for Jesus to save him so Jesus reached out His hand and pulled him up. They both got into the boat, and then the winds died down (Matt 14:22–33). That's how faith is. Faith is not just saying you believe. Faith is living. Faith is knowing that on our own we will sink. Faith is keeping our eyes fixed on Jesus Christ and giving our life over to His hands. When we look away and when we start doing things our own way, we loose that connection with God and start to sink. God uses the storms of life to show us that doing things our way will result in us sinking. Yet by turning to Him; by keeping our eyes fixed on Him, we are protected and grow closer to God.

JUDGMENT OF THE JUST: LOVE

Jesus gave us a new commandment. He tells us that we are to love one another as He has loved us. By this, all will know that we are His followers, if we have love for one another (John 13:34-35, 15:12–17). We fulfill the law of Christ by bearing each other's burdens. The law and the prophets are fulfilled when we love our neighbor as ourselves; when we do onto others as we want them to do to us (Gal 6:1–2; Matt 7:12; Luke 6:31). Our culture today has a warped sense of what love is. When we fall in love, too often it's lust or infatuation. We love our families, bunnies, chocolate, and sitcoms. We show more concern for animals and the environment than we show the homeless. Instead of loving others, we're bombarded with advertisements and broadcasts centered on loving ourselves. Yet with all that, God's message of love is universally understood from generation to generation and across cultures. If we consider how we want to be treated and loved, we know and understand how God wants us to treat others. All the commandments pertaining to our relationship with others are summed up in loving our neighbor as ourselves (Gal 5:14; James 2:8). Love does no harm to a neighbor; therefore love is the fulfillment of the law (Rom 13:8–10).

Jesus tells us that a greater love has no one than to lay down their life for a friend. He died for us, so we should have the same love for each other; that we are willing to lay down our lives for each other. Jesus gave us the perfect example of love to follow. He became a man and gave up His life so that we could be one with God again (1 John 3:16–19). We are to walk in His love as He loved us (Eph 5:2). With this in mind, we should always hold our soldiers, police officers, firefighters, and anyone else that puts their lives in danger to protect us in high regard, and honor them when they die in service to us. Their sacrifice for us brings glory to God.

Love is a fruit of the Holy Spirit living in us, so we should abound in love, being knit together in love, and encourage each other (Gal 5:22–23; Col 2:2). Our consolation in Christ, our comfort of love, our fellowship of the Spirit, and our affection and mercy result from being like-minded in love (Phil 2:1–4). God's light abides in us, and His love is perfected in us as the Holy Spirit teaches us to love our brother. Our love for the brethren is a sincere love like the love we have for our own brother (Col 3:12–14; Phil 1:9–11; 1 Thess 3:12–13, 4:9; 1 Peter 1:22, 2:17, 3:8–9; 1 John 2:10, 3:11, 14). Love is our bond of perfection and covers a multitude of sins (1 Peter 4:8). We are born of God and know God if we love one another (1 John 4:7–12).

It's easy for us to love those who love us; even evil people do that. We are called to love those who are our enemies, to give without expecting anything in return, to be kind to the unthankful and evil, and to be merciful just as God is merciful (Luke 6:32–36; Matt 5:43–47). This is a tall order. It's easy (or should I say easier) to love family, friends, and people whom we like or like us. For all of us, our own love will only take us this far. God wants more than that from His people. We are to love those who hate us or hurt us. We cannot do this of our own abilities. It takes God's Spirit living within us to bring about this transformation in our hearts. Stephen was a good example for us of this love for those who hurt us. When he was being stoned by the Jews for his belief in Jesus Christ, he cried out to God to forgive the people stoning him. He then died (Acts 7:57–60).

The young lawyer that asked Jesus which was the greatest commandment wanted to make himself right with God. He asked Jesus who He considered to be his neighbor. Jesus replied by telling him the parable of the good Samaritan. Everyone ignored or walked by the half-dead man in the parable, except the Samaritan man (by the way, Samaritans were considered no better than dogs to the Jews). The Samaritan man saw the hurt man and had compassion on him. He bandaged his wounds and poured oil and wine on them. He then brought him to an inn, and paid the innkeeper to take care of him until he returned. Jesus used this example to tell the lawyer who his neighbor was (Luke 10:29–37). Our neighbor is everyone. There are no social, economic, national, or cultural exceptions. We are all God's children, so we are all each other's neighbors.

If someone compels us to go one mile with them, go two (Matt 5:41–42). Give to those who ask, love your enemies, bless those who curse you, do good to those who hate you, and pray for those who spitefully use and persecute you. When others are in need, we should provide for that need. When someone is hungry, give them food; when someone is thirsty, give them drink; when someone is a stranger, take them in; when someone is in need of clothing, give them clothes; when someone is sick, visit them; when someone is in prison come to them. Love without hypocrisy; be kindly affectionate to one another; in honor, give preference to one another; rejoice with those who rejoice, and weep with those who weep (Rom 12:9–21; Matt 25:35–40). If food makes your brother stumble, never eat that food in their presence (1 Cor 8:13). Again, all of God's expectations for us in love can be summed up by loving our neighbors as ourselves. When we are in need, we want people to come alongside us and help us, so we should be willing to do the same for others. We always want people to be accepting of us and to not offend us, so we should be willing to do the same for others.

God's desire for us is that we always be there to help and support each other. When we come together to worship God, we are also coming together to support one another in order to stir up love and good works (Heb 10:24–25). We are to serve each other in love. If our desire is to lead our brothers, we must serve them (Gal 5:13; Matt 20:25–28). Jesus, in a very profound way, teaches us to have a heart to serve. In the culture of His day, people wore sandals and walked on dirt roads, so their feet would become very dirty. It was customary for the lowest person in the household to wash the feet of guests when they entered the home. Jesus, our God and creator of all things, washed the feet of each of His followers on the night before He gave his life for us. He told them to serve others as He was serving them (John 13:14–17). If you've never taken part in a foot washing ceremony, I suggest you do some day. Typically, you wash the feet of another person and then they wash your feet. It's a very humbling experience that creates a bond of service between you and the person whose feet you are washing and a bond of love between you and the person washing your feet. When we serve others, we are doing the service for the Lord (1 Tim 6:2; Eph 6:7–8).

Eventually, faith will not be needed. We will be with God and see Him face-to-face, so there will be no need for us to believe in what we can't see. For us in this age, faith is what God expects, and faith is what saves us. In the age to come, faith will be done away with, and what will remain is love. We are nothing without love. Love suffers long and is kind; love does not envy; love does not parade itself, is not puffed up; does not behave rudely, does not seek its own, is not provoked, thinks no evil; does not rejoice in iniquity, but rejoices in the truth; bears all things, believes all things, hopes all things, endures all things. Everything else will eventually go away or fail, but love never fails. As followers of Jesus Christ, we need faith, hope, and love, but the greatest is love (1 Cor 13:2–13).

JUDGMENT OF THE UNJUST

DISBELIEF: AN EXAMPLE TO OTHERS

What happens with the people God resurrects at the second resurrection? We've already been given the picture of God resurrecting mankind and bringing them all back to physical life. They will be put back in their own lands. This suggests that physical life as we know it today will exist for those people again. They will eat, sleep, work, play, and till the soil and raise crops—all the things we do today. The main difference during this time will be that God's kingdom will be firmly established on earth. God's government will be ruling mankind. The results of God's leading will be evident and well established in society since Jesus Christ, and His followers will have ruled over the earth for one thousand years. God will resurrect the dead and reveal Himself to all mankind and make an everlasting covenant with them.

Scripture tells us that all the angels who sinned were delivered into chains of darkness to be reserved for judgment.

The ungodly ancient world that Noah lived in was not spared, but destroyed by the flood. The cities of Sodom and Gomorrah were turned to ashes and condemned to destruction. All this was done by God as an example to those who would afterward live ungodly lives (2 Peter 2:4–10). We are also told that our good works and honorable conduct serve as examples to the ungodly. When they observe our behavior, they may glorify God in the day of visitation (1 Peter 2:12).

Jesus tells us that if we do not believe that He is the Anointed One, we will die in our sins. We are condemned because we do not believe in Him. Our condemnation is that the light has come into the world, yet we love darkness rather than light. Everyone practicing evil hates the light because it exposes their deeds (John 3:18–21). Those who hear the words of Jesus and do not believe them but reject Jesus are judged by the words He spoke (John 6:35–36).

Jesus also told those who don't believe in Him that they don't believe because they aren't His sheep. His sheep hear His voice and follow Him, but they don't follow Him because they aren't His sheep (John 8:24, 10:25–30, 12:47–48). Paul adds that they didn't receive the love of the truth, so God sends them strong delusion that they may believe the lie (2 Thess 2:9–12). It seems like there may be a contradiction here because those that don't believe are judged for that disbelief, yet they don't believe because they're not Jesus's sheep. There is no contradiction here. We will see why this is when we talk later about our calling.

JUDGMENT OF THE ANCIENT PEOPLE

Jesus tells us that it will be more tolerable for the people of Sodom and Gomorrah in the day of judgment than it will be for those cities where Jesus walked and spent time teaching and healing (Matt 10:15, 11:23–24; Mark 6:11; Luke 10:10–12). That's because they were given the opportunity to know Him, and they rejected that opportunity. If God had given the cities of Sodom and Gomorrah the same opportunity to know Jesus Christ as He gave the cities of that time; if Jesus would have performed His mighty works in Sodom and Gomorrah, they would have repented and be here today. Do you realize what this is saying? The people of Sodom and Gomorrah will be resurrected in the second resurrection—the resurrection of judgment. They were so wicked that God totally destroyed them. Yet those people will not be destroyed or thrown into hell as we've been taught. Rather, Jesus tells us that their judgment will be more tolerable for them than the judgment of the people of Jesus's day will be. God had not given them the opportunity to know Jesus Christ and witness the miracles that followed Him. If God had, they would have repented. God chose to use Sodom and Gomorrah as an example to others who would live sinful lives, but in the resurrection, they will have the opportunity to know Jesus Christ. Their judgment will be more tolerable for them than the judgment for the cities where Jesus Christ walked and taught. As we read before, this completely aligns with what we find in prophecy concerning the people of Sodom. God does not destroy them, but rather, they are given to Israel as an inheritance. This also aligns with what Scripture tells us of the judgment: each person will be judged according to the knowledge they were given and their works.

Jesus makes identical statements about other ancient cities and people that did not follow God. He tells us that it will be more tolerable for Tyre and Sidon in the day of judgment than for the people of His time. Tyre and Sidon would have repented in sackcloth and ashes if the mighty works done by Jesus were done in those cities (Matt 11:21–22; Luke 10:13–16).

The people of Nineveh will rise up in the judgment with Jesus's generation and condemn it because they repented at the preaching of Jonah; and indeed Jesus is much greater than Jonah. Realize that Nineveh was a wicked city like Sodom. Their wickedness came up to God just like the wickedness of Sodom. God's intention was to destroy the city just as He did with Sodom and Gomorrah. The only difference between Sodom and Gomorrah and Nineveh was that God chose to send Jonah to Nineveh. He let the people of Nineveh know what would happen if they didn't change. When the people heard Jonah speak, they immediately asked God for forgiveness and changed their ways. As a result, God did not destroy Nineveh (Jonah 1:2, 4:10–11; Matt 12:41; Luke 11:29–30, 32).

The queen of Sheba came to see the wisdom of Solomon. She recognized that the God of Solomon delighted in him, setting him on the throne of Israel. She was able to say that the Lord has loved Israel forever, therefore, He made Solomon king to do justice and make right decisions (1 Kings 10:4–9). She had no relationship with God, yet she understood that there is a Creator God, and He was greatly blessing Solomon and Israel. The queen of Sheba will rise in the judgment with the people of Jesus's time and condemn them, because she recognized Solomon's wisdom was from God, and Jesus is much greater than Solomon was (Matt 12:42; Luke 11:31). In all these cases, the people mentioned arise in the second resurrection—the resurrection of judgment. They are not destroyed, but they are judged according to their works. Therefore, their judgment will be much less severe than the people who were exposed to Jesus and His mighty works, yet did not change their ways.

You can see a consistent pattern that is established in the Bible regarding judgment of the just and unjust. God gives each of us everything we have and then holds us accountable for how we used those gifts in our lives. To those that have been given much, much is expected. To those who have been given little, less is expected.

JUDGMENT ACCORDING TO KNOWLEDGE AND WORKS

Jesus told the Jewish leadership that they wouldn't have sinned if they were blinded to the truth of Jesus, or if He had not come and spoken to them. Since He did come to them and they had all the Scriptures that pointed to His coming, they were without excuse. Each person will give an account or be accountable for the knowledge they've been given and how they used that knowledge (John 9:41, 15:22–25). The implication here is that the conditions of your former life (status, spiritual knowledge, heart condition, and behaviors, etc.) will determine what the conditions of life will be like in the resurrection. This thought is further substantiated by Jesus when He said that the servant who knew His will and didn't prepare himself accordingly will be beaten with many stripes, but the servant who didn't know God's will and did things deserving of stripes will be beaten with fewer stripes (Luke 12:46–48). The one willingly disobeys and the other doesn't realize they're doing wrong. Both servants were disobedient to God and take part in the second resurrection. The first rejected God, and the second didn't know God. Both are accountable for their actions, and they are judged based on their knowledge and actions.

There are other scriptures that align with this thought, some stronger in language and others more subtle. Jesus said it would have been good if the man who betrayed Him hadn't been born, and He told the Pharisees they would receive a greater condemnation because they were the religious leaders, and they didn't even recognize Him (Matt 26:24; Mark 14:21; Luke 20:46–47). Jesus also said that those who had more will be giving more, and those who don't have, what they have will be taken away (Matt 25:28–30). Peter tells us that those who know the way to live aligned with God and turn back to their old ways would be better off if they never knew the right way to live (2 Peter 2:20–22). In all these examples, we are told that we will be held accountable for the knowledge we were given. The more the knowledge we've been given, the more sever the judgment will be.

God will render to each of us according to our works or deeds (2 Cor 11:15). For those who are self-seeking and don't obey the truth, they will treasure up indignation, severe troubles, and anguish in the day of wrath in accordance with the hardness and impenitence of their heart (Rom 2:5–10). Our own words will judge us (Luke 19:22–25). God will execute judgment on all the ungodly to convict them of their ungodly deeds (Jude 14–15).

Paul tells us to deliver a sinner to Satan for the destruction of the flesh so that his spirit may be saved in the day of the Lord (1 Cor 5:5; Rev 18:4–8). God is concerned with a change in heart, so God will use this life and the judgment to turn us to Him.

We saw how God will judge the ungodly based on their knowledge. The Scriptures also tell us that judgment will be based on the type of offense. Those who trouble God's people shall be judged for that and be repaid with severe troubles (Gal 5:10; 2 Thess 1:6). Those who teach others to sin shall be called least in the kingdom of God (Matt 5:19). Religious teachers who are hypocrites, devouring widows' houses and making long prayers for a pretense will receive a greater condemnation (Matt 23:14). If someone offends a child, it would be better if a millstone was hung around their neck, and they were thrown into the sea and drowned than to face their judgment (Matt 18:6–7; Mark 9:42; Luke 17:2).

Jesus said that He will deny before the angels of God anyone who denies Him (Luke 12:8–9). He will be ashamed of those who are ashamed of Him and His words (Mark 8:34–38; Luke 9:23–26). Anyone who eats and drinks the Lord's supper in an unworthy manor, eats and drinks judgment unto themselves not discerning the Lord's body (1 Cor 11:29).

If someone has had their hearts opened to God's truth and experienced God's goodness and then falls away, they cannot be renewed again by the sacrifice of Jesus. Their actions bring shame upon Jesus's sacrifice (Heb 6:4–6). Anyone who speaks irreverently against the Holy Spirit will not be forgiven (Luke 12:10). If we sin willfully after we have received knowledge of the truth, there no longer remains a sacrifice for sins but a certain fearful expectation of judgment and fiery indignation. How much worse punishment, do you suppose, will those who disrespect the covenant made in Jesus's blood receive? God tells us that vengeance is His, and He will judge His people, so it's a fearful thing for those who sin against the Holy Spirit this way to fall into the hands of the living God (Heb 10:26–31). The point here is that anyone who receives the Holy Spirit and then rejects such a wonderful gift will not be forgiven. We don't know if this would actually happen, or if it's meant to be a stern warning to not take such a wonderful gift so lightly. It's hard to imagine this actually happen. However, we can only go by what the passages are telling us. They will rise in the second resurrection and be judged according to everything they've been given just like everyone else. Except in their case, the judgment will be the most severe of anyone.

Jesus uses the example of settling a dispute with others to teach a principle in the judgment. If we refuse to make peace with our enemy, we will go before the judge and be thrown into prison until we pay back every last penny (Luke 12:56–59). God's punishment is not there to destroy, but to turn our hearts to Him. In all of these Scriptures, God is telling us that the conditions of this life will determine the conditions of life at the second resurrection. It would be better for some (from their perspective) if they hadn't lived. Some will be beaten with many stripes, and some will be last, but the point for all mankind is that they will live, and God will use their resurrected lives to turn them to Him.

For those of us whom God is drawing to Himself today, the interaction between God and us is very similar. We all can identify a point in our lives when God started calling us to Him. For some of us, our lives may have changed immediately. For others, we tried to run from God or recognized the need for Him but resisted giving up our old ways. In all our cases, God never gave up on us. I like using the analogy of a parent raising their child. As a parent, you know the character you want your child to develop, so throughout their life you're disciplining them, nurturing them, coaching them, and teaching them so that they end up being a mature responsible adult. How much more so with God. For those in the second resurrection, God will judge them for the behaviors, circumstances, and actions of their past life. Then God will give them a new life with new conditions and open their hearts to Him and mold their character.

ETERNAL JUDGMENT

Eternal judgment is a doctrine that we find throughout the Old and New Testaments. It is so basic to our beliefs that Paul refers to it as one of the elementary principles of Christ (Heb 6:1–2). The doctrine is typically written similar to this: We believe that unbelievers rise at the second resurrection to appear at the Great White Throne judgment where they shall be cast into the lake of fire, suffering everlasting punishment. Some churches add everlasting torment in hell to the description. There's much to be said about our fundamental beliefs on this topic outside the scope of this book, so I focus on those things the Bible tells us about eternal judgment that are relevant to this study.

Scripture is filled with descriptions of this judgment of the unjust. Eternal judgment is referred to as everlasting punishment and eternal condemnation or the resurrection of condemnation (Matt 25:46; Mark 3:29; John 5:28–29). The unjust are condemned, so they are consumed and perish; they perish in their own corruption, they perish forever, and they vanish or melt away (Job 4:9, 20:5–7; Ps 1:4–6, 37:20, 112:10; 2 Thess 2:10, 12; 2 Peter 2:12). They are punished and destroyed so that all memory of them is gone. Their future is cut off and their names are blotted out forever. Their destruction is forever; it's an everlasting destruction from the face of the Lord (Job 31:3, 11–12; Ps 5:6, 9:5, 37:38, 55:23, 92:7, 145:20; Pro 13:12–14, 15:11; Isa 1:28, 26:14; Matt 7:13–14; Luke 9:25; Phil 3:19; 2 Thess 1:9; Heb 10:39; 2 Peter 2:6, 3:7).

We are told that the wicked shall be silent in darkness; that blackness and darkness forever are reserved for them (1 Sam 2:9; 2 Peter 2:17). There will be weeping and gnashing of teeth when they are cast into outer darkness (Matt 22:13, 25:30).

Scripture often uses fire to symbolize the sentence for the unjust. God will judge all humans by fire and by His sword (Ps 140:10; Isa 66:16–17). The unjust will be cast into a fire, and it shall burn them until they are stubble (Isa 47:14). God will rain coals upon the wicked; fire and brimstone and burning wind (Ps 11:6). God will burn them up with unquenchable fire—a fire will consume them (Job 20:26; Isa 50:11, 66:24; Matt 3:10–12; Heb 10:27). As withered branches are gathered together and burned, so shall the unjust be cast out, thrown into a fire, and burned (Matt 13:30; John 15:6; Heb 6:8).

In the New Testament, Jesus used the word *gehenna*, which was a valley outside the city of Jerusalem, to describe the judgment for the unjust (Matt 5:22, 29–30, 18:8–9, Mark 9:43–48). Gehenna was basically used as a garbage dump where fires were always burning to eliminate trash. He said those who would not repent would be in danger of this gehenna fire. Jesus also said that this everlasting fire of judgment was prepared for the devil and his angels, and the cursed would be thrown into it as well (Matt 25:41).

Malachi foretold of a day coming, burning like an oven, and all the wicked will burn and be stubble. They will be ashes under the soles of your feet (Mal 4:1–3). John, in the book of Revelation refers to this oven as the lake of fire. Anyone not found written in the book of life was cast into the lake of fire. It's a lake that burns with fire and brimstone. It's also known as the second death (the first being our physical death) (Rev 20:14–15, 21:8). The angels of God will gather up all who offend or practice lawlessness and cast them into the furnace of fire (Matt 13:40–42, 49–50).

The Scriptures are also clear in telling us that the wicked will be no more (Ps 37:9-11; Pro 10:25). God does not preserve the life of the wicked; their lamp will be put out (Job 36:6; Pro 24:20). The light of their lamp indeed goes out and the flame of their fire does not shine. The memory of the wicked also perishes. The memory of them will be gone (Job 18:5-21, 24:20; Ezek 21:31–32). God will blot out their name from under heaven and the book of the living (Deut 29:20; Ps 69:28). The Scriptures are also clear in telling us that God put eternity in our hearts (Ecc 3:11). He put the desire in each of us to live forever. You can see then that there's a conflict here that motivates some early on in life but ultimately will motivate everyone. God puts the desire to live eternally within us, yet anyone who refuses to turn to Him will be blotted out of existence.

We are all mortal, and it's God and God alone who has immortality (Job 4:17, 10:5; Rom 6:12; 2 Cor 4:11; 1 Tim 6:16–17; Heb 7:8). We put on immortality by receiving the Holy Spirit from God when we repent and believe in Jesus Christ and His sacrifice for our sins (1 Cor 15:53-54; 1 Tim 6:12). The Holy Spirit is our seal, our promise, and our guarantee of eternal life (John 3:5–6, 4:13–14, 6:27; 2 Cor 1:21–22; Eph 1:13–14, 4:30). The same spirit that raised Jesus Christ from the dead will raise our mortal bodies (Rom 8:9–11). God will not sustain a life that ultimately rejects Him. The question is can anyone resist God (Rom 9:19)?

GOD'S CALLING

ISRAEL CALLED BY GOD

In the book of Acts, chapter seven, Stephen goes before the Sanhedrin (the Jewish leadership) to defend the way. Filled with the Holy Spirit, Stephen recounts Israel's history, starting with God's calling of Abram (God later changes his name to Abraham) while he was still in Mesopotamia (Acts 7:2–8). God chose Abraham and told him to leave his home and travel to a distant land that God would later give to his descendents. God made a covenant with Abraham to give him the Promised Land (Neh 9:7–8). Abraham believed God's promise to him even though he had never seen the land, was without child, and he and his wife Sarah were beyond the child bearing years (Rom 4:1–3). Abraham's faith and not anything he had done, put him in right standing with God (Rom 4:13–15).

God loved Abraham, his son Isaac, and his son Jacob (renamed Israel by God) (Deut 4:37–38). Therefore, He chose Israel's descendents, the twelve tribes of Israel (Israel had twelve sons), to be a special treasure to Him above all other people (Deut 14:2; Ps 135:4). God brought Israel out of Egypt with His mighty power (Israel had essentially become slave labor to the Egyptians), drove out the people who lived in the land God had promised, and brought them into it (Gen 45:7; Deut 7:6–8). Again, God's choosing of Israel was not based on anything they had done, but based on God's love for them and the oath He had made to their fathers.

God blessed Israel in a tremendous way that He had never blessed any other people. God spoke to Israel, showed Himself through amazing signs, and led them out of bondage using miraculous means to free them. God did this so they could know that our Lord is God, and there is none other besides Him (Deut 4:32–40). This should have been all the motivation Israel would need to obey God, but obviously it wasn't.

Now, back to Stephen's recounting of Israel's history. Stephen goes on to tell the Jewish leadership that they were stiff-necked, just as their fathers were. Throughout Israel's history, they rejected God, His prophets, and ultimately Jesus, the Just One (Acts 7:51–53). God warned Israel over and over again that there would be consequences to their disobedience. God told them that disobedience would lead to them being scattered among the nations and few in number (Deut 4:25–28, 28:62). Israel's sin was a sin of disbelief. Israel tried to fulfill all the requirements of the law through their works so they didn't attain a proper standing with God because they didn't seek it through faith (Rom 9:31–33).

However, God did not turn completely against Israel, nor did He reject His promise to Abraham (Deut 4:29–31). Even though Israel rejected God throughout their history, God remained true to His promise to Abraham by maintaining a remnant of Israel (Isa 1:9). God continuously reserved a remnant for Himself of those who did not turn away from Him (Isa 46:3–4). Through this remnant that God upheld, He would fulfill all the promises made to Abraham. Realize that when God made His covenant with Abraham, there were the physical blessings of innumerable descendents and a homeland attached to it, but there was also the promise that all mankind would be blessed through Abraham (Gen 12:1–3).

That blessing to all mankind through Abraham was in Jesus, the Anointed One. That's why the books of Matthew and Luke show the physical genealogy of Jesus through Joseph and Mary, respectively, being preserved through this remnant of Abraham's descendents (Matt 1:1–17; Luke 3:23–38). This remnant also provided servants of God (prophets) whom God used to announce the coming of His grace through Jesus. Their purpose was to testify of the suffering of the Anointed One and the glories that would follow for Him. Through their preserved messages, they also served as ministers to all those who would come after them (Gen 12:3; Luke 24:25-27, 44–45; Heb 1:1–4; 1 Pet 1:6–12).

These prophets did not have it easy. They were persecuted, stoned, and killed for the message they brought (Matt 23:37; Luke 13:34; Acts 7:51–53). There's a parable that Jesus told in the book of Mark that summarizes Israel's relationship with the prophets and Jesus. The owner of a vineyard repeatedly sent servants to receive fruit from the vinedresser. The servants were beaten, stoned, and some were killed by the vinedresser. The owner finally sent his son to them, hoping that the vinedresser would respect his son. The son was killed and cast out of the vineyard (Mark 12:1–11).

Just like Adam and Eve before them, Israel didn't accept God ruling over their lives. They rejected God and any of His messengers. They tried to attain a right standing with God on their own, apart from God. They refused to believe and trust in God's way for them. Israel stumbled at that stumbling stone; that is, they didn't believe in Jesus Christ (Rom 9:31–33). By the way, at the end of Stephen's defense of the way, he too was stoned and killed (Acts 7:54–60).

God had every right to totally reject Israel. With all of the ways Israel rejected God, they were deserving of any judgment brought upon them (Ezra 9:13–15). However, God also used the remnant He sustained to demonstrate His unmerited favor toward Israel. Israel was not able to attain a good standing with God through their actions or means. The only way they could be right with God was by God showing them unmerited favor (Rom 9:27–28, 11:1–6). It was God's design to keep a remnant through grace, and the rest of Israel was blinded (Rom 9:18).

Paul tells us it was necessary that the word of God should be spoken to Israel first, but since Israel rejected it, the word of God was spoken to the rest of mankind. God sent Paul to be a light to mankind and to take the teaching of how God would restore our relationship with Him to the ends of the earth. Since Israel rejected God, He gave them a spirit of stupor, eyes that they should not see, and ears that they should not hear (Acts 3:26, 13:46–47; Rom 11:7–10).

In the book of Hebrews we find a description of this remnant God has been preserving from the creation of mankind until Jesus's time that believed the promises of God and were made right with God through their faith. All of their circumstances were different, yet they all were united by faith. All of them died not having received the promises, but having seen them afar off, they were assured of them and embraced them. They all believed that their reward was not of this earth but was a spiritual blessing (Heb 11). This remnant of believers surrounds us and witness to us of the same spiritual blessings we have in Jesus, the Anointed One (Rom 3:21–22; Heb 12:1). It's interesting to note that they too suffered persecution and death for their witness.

So we see then that even though Israel had totally rejected God, God maintained a remnant of Abraham's descendents to fulfill the physical promises to Israel, provide a lineage for the spiritual blessing of Jesus, provide prophets to announce the future coming of the Anointed One, demonstrated God's grace, and establish witnesses who lived by faith as examples to us who would follow. God had a specific purpose for His remnant. It wasn't God's plan at that time to draw all mankind to Himself. Rather God allowed mankind to continue on the path we had chosen, and called a remnant to further and serve His plan.

GOD'S PEOPLE TODAY

God's people today are a cross section of mankind. There are no cultural, political, social, or economic barriers that separate us from each other and God. We are called the firstfruits of God's creation (James 1:18; Rev 14:4). Remember earlier where Jesus was referred to as the firstborn or firstfruit of those who rise from the dead. This concept was familiar to Israel because God, in giving Israel the sacrificial system, ordained that Israel bring the firstfruits of all their produce to God as an offering. Now God is calling His people today the firstfruits of His family. We are the firstfruits or first produce of a great harvest (Rom 8:29–30). We are not that great harvest itself, but the firstfruits or beginnings of that harvest.

God has made Himself known to few. Jesus said the Father has hidden Himself and His word from the wise and prudent and revealed Himself to babes because it seemed good to God. No one knows who the Son is except the Father, and no one knows who the Father is except the Son, and the one to whom the Son wills to reveal Him to. Jesus told His disciples privately that their eyes were blessed for seeing the things they saw because many prophets and kings desired to see what they had seen (Luke 10:21–24). He often spoke in parables because it was given to the disciples to know the mysteries of the kingdom of God but not the Jewish leadership (Matt 13:11–17; Luke 8:10).

What we take away from all this is that at this time, during this age, God is working with a type of remnant of His people—His firstfruits. Jesus used the parable of the sower to explain how His word is received in people today. When anyone hears the word and doesn't understand it, the wicked one comes and snatches it away from their heart (Matt 13:18–19). It's not that these people are not wise or mighty or noble enough to understand (1 Cor 1:26–29). Rather, it's that they are blinded by God (Rom 11:7). God calls the foolish, the weak, and the despised to put to shame those that are wise, mighty, and noble so that no flesh shall glory in His presence. Those that don't understand the word of God were not given to Jesus Christ by the Father, so they cannot know the truth (John 17:2–3; 1 Thess 5:9).

Continuing on with the parable, anyone who has no root hears the word and immediately receives it with joy, yet they endure only for a while. For when tribulation or persecution arises because of the word, immediately they stumble (Matt 13:20–21). Remember how God's remnant was persecuted, and many were killed? Those called by God today will experience the same treatment. God opens the understanding of some to His word, but they are not chosen for His special purpose today, so they quickly fall away when times get difficult. Jesus had many people that liked hearing the message He was giving, yet because they were not chosen by the Father, they had no root and soon stopped following Him (Matt 22:14; John 6:60–67).

Back to the parable, those who are unfruitful hear the word, but the cares of this world and the deceitfulness of riches choke out the word (Matt 13:22). It's only those who are chosen by God that are appointed to bear fruit that remains. They are chosen by God for a specific purpose at this time (John 6:70–71, 15:16, 19; Acts 13:48).

The parable ends by telling us that those who hear the word and understand it bear fruit abundantly—some a hundredfold, some sixty, some thirty (Matt 13:23). These are the people God has called with a special calling according to His purpose (John 14:6; 2 Tim 1:9). All those that God has chosen and given to Jesus Christ will by no means be cast out (John 6:37). God chose His elect from the beginning to have a restored relationship with Him by giving them His Spirit and a belief in the truth (2 Thess 2:13–14). Those given to Jesus are His elect according to the foreknowledge of God the Father (1 Peter 1:2). God foreknew, and predetermined them to be conformed to the image of His Son. Moreover those whom God predetermined, these He also called, made acceptable, and glorified. God chose them in Him before the foundation of the world that they should be special and without blame before Him in love. God predetermined them to adoption as sons by Jesus Christ to Himself according to the good pleasure of His will (Acts 2:39; Rom 8:29–30; Eph 1:3–6).

As we saw earlier, the prophets proclaimed and foretold of the coming of the Anointed One. That was their main commission from God (Acts 10:42–43). God's people today have a similar commission. Prior to leaving the earth after His resurrection, Jesus told His followers to go to the ends of the earth proclaiming the good news to all nations as a witness (Matt 24:14; Mark 13:10, 16:15; Luke 24:47–48; Acts 1:8, 26:16). They had been with Him throughout His ministry so they knew Jesus and could speak of Him from their experiences with Him. The good news was to be brought to God's people Israel first, and then taken to the rest of mankind (Acts 13:46–47). Those of us who have come after are to proclaim this same good news, only we are proclaiming it from the perspective of believing God's word as passed down to us by the prophets and followers of Jesus, and not from the perspective of being with Him during His ministry.

The result of proclaiming the good news to mankind is that some (those God is calling) believe and see the Anointed One as the power and wisdom of God, yet most would see it as foolishness. However, even though they reject Jesus they would be convicted of their rebellion against God (Mark 16:15–16; 1 Cor 1:22–25). Those who reject the good news will be individually addressed by God in His time and manner.

Those who believe need to be nurtured and taught (Matt 28:19–20). That's the second commission for God's people today; to help, teach, and support other followers of Jesus (Acts 26:16–18, 28:30–31; Rom 10:14–15). God's design for His family is for us to learn and grow together. It's a life-long journey we are on that makes us one with God and one with each other. We are united in Jesus, the Anointed One (Eph 4:11–13).

Paul uses the human body as an analogy to describe how God's people interact with each other and support each other. The body has many members (eyes, hands, head, feet, etc.) that all work together so that the body will function properly and completely. Each of us in God's family has different skills, strengths, and weaknesses that all work together to support each other and fulfill the work that God has for us (1 Cor 12:20–26).

Finally, God also wants His people to be an example to others. Jesus uses salt and light as metaphors for our relationship with our fellow man (Matt 5:13–16). Just as salt brings out the flavor in food, we are to bring out the best in others—to not judge them and be critical of them, but to look for, bring out, and focus on the good in them. Just as light shines forth in the darkness and provides us with a clear way to go, the way we live our life should illuminate God's love for us and all His creation. Those called into God's service today should be that salt and light to others.

CHOOSE LIFE

Our teaching usually stops at this point. We talk about being called but the idea of predestination causes division. The idea of free will has dominated our teaching, so predestination is a kind of slippery slope, especially since we don't fully understand God's plan. We also get hung up on the notion that if God predestined some for eternal life, then everyone else is predestined to eternal punishment. This thought is confusing to most, especially those who know God's love, mercy, and grace in their own lives. Paul takes this idea head on by first telling us we have no right to question God. What if God, wanting to show His power and wrath, endured those prepared for destruction, and made known His mercy on those prepared before hand for glory (Rom 9:22–24)? The potter has power over the clay, to decide if one vessel is made for honor and another for dishonor (Rom 9:20–21). Paul is not saying that God's will is to create some people for destruction. Rather, he's telling us we need to understand our place and not question our Creator based on human reasoning. We should always look to God and His word for answers.

There's an important distinction we need to make between our God given attribute of choice and God's calling. The lesson we learn from Adam and Eve, and Israel is that mankind wants to decide right and wrong for ourselves and we resist any dependence on God. God has allowed us to go our own way and in fact has hardened our hearts to knowing Him because of that. So you see, the issues we face in the world are our issue; issues brought on by us choosing to go our own way.

When we talk about our calling, God's word tells us over and over again that it's God who draws us to Him. It's God who opens our hearts to know Him, and seek Him. God chooses us in the manor and timing He decides. God's calling stems from His grace; the unmerited favor He shows us. There is nothing we can do to be right with God. We cannot take credit or boast about our calling because as mentioned previously, our hearts desire apart from God is to go our own way. Free will has absolutely nothing to do with our calling, or us choosing God. God chooses us!

When we read about predestination in God's word, it's always in the context of when and how God decides to work in our lives, for the specific purposes He has for us. God chose Abraham, He chose all the prophets, He chose His disciples, He chooses who He will call in this lifetime, and He chooses those He will call in the resurrection. God is sovereign over His creation and will use each and every one of us to further

His plan in the manner He decides. So when considering your calling, don't even dare to think that you chose God. You didn't, He chose you. Otherwise, your being saved is not a matter of faith through grace; it's a matter of works through choosing. We'll talk in depth about God's grace later.

Where our free will; our God given ability to choose comes into play is after God draws us to Him. Anyone who has had their life transformed by God knows that our walk with God is a journey (probably with no end in sight). You know the old saying, "it's not the destination that's important; it's the journey".

There's a big word used in the Bible that refers to this journey. It's called sanctification. It simply means being purified. God's desire for those He calls is for them to be purified and cleansed so that they may be one with Him and to prepare them for His service (1 Thess 4:3, 7–8; 2 Tim 2:21; Titus 2:14; Heb 2:11).

We take part in the process of transforming our lives. The Bible uses action words to describe our part in the process. We put off the old self; our old conduct; our sinful ways. We put to death our earthly desires (Eph 4:20–31; Col 3:5–9). We are to distance ourselves from the childish ways we lived prior to being called (1 Cor 13:11–12). We are to seek and set our minds on the things that are above (Col 3:1–4). We flee from youthful lusts and avoid foolish disputes, while pursuing a right relationship with others and walking in the light (Eph 5:8–10; 2 Tim 2:22–23; Heb 12:14; 1 John 1:7–9). We cleanse ourselves from all filthiness (2 Cor 7:1).

All this is done by allowing God to rule our hearts and the word of Jesus to dwell richly in us (Col 3:15–17). Our spirit becomes renewed by putting on the new person, renewed in knowledge according to the image of God (Eph 4:23–24). We put on and take up the whole armor of God, and put on the fruits of the Spirit (Gal 5:22–23; Eph 6:10–13; Col 3:10–14).

Let's be clear, the changes in our lives are accomplished by God's Spirit, living in us (Rom 15:15–16; 1 Cor 6:11; 1 Thess 5:23; Heb 10:14–15; 1 Pet 1:2). Our part is to submit to God's will for us and allow His Spirit to guide our lives (John 16:12–14, 17:17; 2 Thess 2:13). God's Spirit living in us opens our heart to understand His word, teaches us all things and guides us into all truth (John 14:26). As we discussed previously, God is purifying us in the faith we have in Jesus, and in the love we have for our fellow man (Acts 15:8–9, 26:17–18; Phil 1:3–11).

ALL MANKIND CALLED BY GOD

All mankind, God's creation, was subjected to futility and the bondage of corruption (our physical bodies that eventually wear out and die). The whole creation groans and labors with birth pains together until now. God will deliver His creation into the glorious liberty of the children of God. Not only that, but even those of us who have the firstfruits of the Spirit groan within ourselves, eagerly waiting for the adoption, the changing of our body (Rom 8:20–23). So you see then that even though we many not realize it, all of God's creation is longing for His plan to restore our relationship with Him to be fulfilled. We all want world peace and universal harmony between us, our God, and His creation. The problem is we don't know how to achieve it and can't achieve it apart from God.

In telling us that the firstfruits of God's people today are special, Paul goes on to say that the rest of the crop is also special (Rom 11:15–16). God has committed Israel to disobedience that He might have mercy on all of us. God used Israel's disbelief to draw the rest of mankind to Him, but ultimately, all Israel will also be saved (Rom 11:23–26). The gifts and the calling of God are irrevocable. Mankind was once disobedient to God, yet has found mercy and grace through Israel's disobedience. Conversely, God's mercy shown to mankind will also be shown to Israel. Paul summarizes God's plan, proclaiming that the richness and depth of the wisdom and knowledge of God and His judgments are beyond searching and His ways beyond finding out (Rom 11:29–36)! God is the God of all mankind, not just Israel and not just people who are not Israel. God makes no distinction (Rom 10:10–13). In the near future, whoever calls on the name of the Lord shall be saved. God's ultimate plan is to draw all mankind back to Himself (Acts 2:21).

In the Old Testament, we find prophecies for the Holy Spirit being poured out (Pro 1:23). Isaiah paints a beautiful picture of God's Spirit being poured out from on high. The wilderness becomes a fruitful field, and the fruitful field becomes a forest (Isa 32:15). God's Spirit is poured out on Israel's descendents and His blessings on their offspring (Isa 44:3, 45:8). God will pour down everything we need to have a restored relationship with Him. One of the most familiar prophecies regarding the giving of the Holy Spirit comes from the book of Joel. He tells us that God will pour out His Spirit on all flesh. A time is coming when whoever calls on the name of the Lord shall be saved (Joel 2:28–32). When the Holy Spirit was given on Pentecost, Peter stood up and spoke to those present. He quoted the prophecy from Joel, telling them that the things they were witnessing were because this prophecy was being fulfilled (Acts 2:14–18, 38). God at that time gave the Holy Spirit to those who repented and believed, fulfilling a portion of the prophecy. The rest of the prophecy, that all flesh would receive the Holy Spirit has yet to be fulfilled.

You may be thinking there's a contradiction here because we're told that anyone calling on God will receive His Spirit, and yet Jesus told us that it's God who calls us to Him. There is no contradiction here because there are two different ages involved. In this age as we've seen previously, God calls those He has chosen to Himself. In the ages to come, God will call everyone to Him and pour out His Spirit on all mankind. If you believe differently, that God truly is calling all mankind to Himself today, then God must be constrained by time and chance, because there are many millions of people who still haven't been exposed to the truth of God, or clearly haven't had the truths of God's words opened to them. How do you reconcile what you believe with what you see every day in the world, and what the Bible tells us about our calling? If you look at all the passages on our calling and the pouring out of God's Spirit, it becomes clear that God has stages to His plan to give the Holy Spirit as a gift to mankind. Again, in this age God is drawing a remnant or firstfruits of His Spirit for a special purpose, and in the ages to come He will pour out His Spirit on the rest of mankind.

There are three annual feasts or festival seasons that God gave to Israel. They are the Feast of Unleavened Bread, the Feast of Harvest (or Weeks, or Firstfruits) during the spring harvest (there were two harvest seasons in the land of Israel) and the Feast of Ingathering (or Tabernacles), during the fall harvest (Ex 23:14–16). There are many opinions on what these feast days mean, but what we know for certain is that they foreshadow God's plan to renew mankind's relationship with Him. Jesus was crucified on the Passover (part of the Feast of Unleavened Bread), and the Holy Spirit was given on Pentecost (Greek name for the Feast of Weeks). Both occurred during the spring harvest. As God's plan is unfolding, the spiritual meaning of each of God's feasts is becoming evident. With this understanding you can start to see why God's people today are referred to as the firstfruits of a great harvest (Rom 8:29–30; James 1:18; Rev 14:4).

There is disagreement on the true meaning of the Feast of Tabernacles, but what we can say with certainty is that the Feast of Tabernacles is the last feast of God, and the last great day is the very last holy day during that feast. The last great day pictures the culmination of God's plan of restoring His relationship with all mankind. That's why Jesus cried out as He did.

> On the last day, that great day of the feast (Feast of Tabernacles), Jesus stood and cried out, saying, "If anyone thirsts, let him come to Me and drink. He who believes in Me, as the Scripture has said, out of his heart will flow rivers of living water." But this He spoke concerning the Spirit, whom those believing in Him would receive; for the Holy Spirit was not yet given because Jesus was not yet glorified.
>
> John 7:37–39

Jesus wasn't inviting all mankind to Himself then, He was telling us what He and the Father have in store for all mankind. God's plan to restore our relationship with Him culminates with God inviting all mankind to Himself.

GOD'S REWARD

GOD'S REWARD FOR ALL MANKIND

God tells us that He has no pleasure in the death of the wicked, but that the wicked turn from their ways and live (Ezek 33:11). God will not cast us off forever. He does not afflict us willingly nor grieve us to crush us. God will show compassion according to the multitude of His mercies (Lam 3:31–36). His ultimate purpose is to turn us to Him, so He puts correction before us then rewards us as we turn back to Him.

Jesus taught that those who have the most sin in their lives will treasure forgiveness much more than those who have little to forgive (Luke 7:47). The rich young leader was keeping all the law since his youth, yet he was putting too much into His riches, so Jesus told Him to sell all he had and follow Him. The young ruler wanted perfection, so Jesus told him what it would take and then told him his treasures would be in heaven. Not only was he consumed by his riches, he had pride in his righteousness, so to him, having to give more was unfair. Didn't he already do enough to have riches in heaven? In his mind, the young rich ruler needed forgiveness for little, so he was unwilling to put in the extra effort to have a closer relationship with God (Mark 10:17–22).

As Jesus sat to eat at the home of a Pharisee, a woman washed Jesus's feet with her tears and wiped them with her hair. She then kissed His feet and anointed them with very expensive oil. The woman had many sins and desired forgiveness. No one else came close to showing the love she showed toward Jesus. To her, being such a sinner had put a huge wall between her and God. Her joy in knowing her relationship with God could be renewed through the forgiveness of Jesus spilled out in much love for Him. Jesus saw her faith and forgave her sins (Luke 7:36–50).

We tend to judge people based on the graveness of their sins. We ask questions like, "How can that person ever be saved?" The point is that we are all sinners, and if it wasn't for God's grace, we would not stand. God's concern is for our future with Him. When you look at the entire passage in Ezekiel, chapter thirty-three, God repeats that same message four times. If a righteous person turns to sin he will die, but if a sinner turns to God he will live (Ezek 33:10–20). God wants every single one of us to turn from evil; to turn to Him and live.

The reward that God promises to those who turn to righteousness is everlasting or eternal life (Dan 12:2-3; Matt

25:46; 1 John 2:25). Eternal life is given to those who hear the words of Jesus Christ and believe in Him, His name, and the Father who sent Him (John 3:14–16, 36, 5:24, 39–40, 6:40, 47; 1 Tim 1:16; 1 John 5:11–13). Jesus gives us understanding to know Him and the Father. We are in God and Jesus Christ; this is eternal life (1 John 5:20). Jesus tells us the water He gives us will become a fountain of water springing up into everlasting life (John 4:13–14). He also tells us that whoever eats His flesh and drinks His blood has eternal life (John 6:54–58). What Jesus is telling us is that when we turn to Him, it's not just in words; we turn to Him for life, for everything to live. We recognize that only through Him and in Him is our being. He gives us everything we need to live and prosper. It is Jesus who has broken down the wall sin has placed between us and God. Jesus Christ's death and resurrection allow us to once again have an intimate relationship with God.

Jesus gives the gift of eternal life to those the Father has given Him. God sets us free from sin and we become servants of God. We belong to God. Jesus uses a shepherd and sheep to describe our relationship with Him. He said He knows His sheep, and His sheep know Him. No one can take us away from Him. When you look at the relationship between a shepherd and his sheep, there's an amazing bond between them, and God uses that bond to describe our relationship with Him when we become His people. Psalm twenty-three is one of my favorite passages in the Bible, because it gives us this wonderful picture of God comforting and providing for all our needs. We have no need to want or fear for we dwell within God's mercy and grace forever (Ps 23:1–6; John 10:27–28, 17:2–3; Rom 6:22–23).

Eternal life is given to those who love God with all their heart, with all their soul, with all their strength, and with all their mind, and love their neighbor as themselves (Luke 10:25–28). It's given to those who patiently continue to do good and seek glory, honor, and immortality (Rom 2:6–7). It's given to those who have left their worldly loves behind for Jesus Christ (Matt 19:29). Anyone losing in this life for Jesus's sake will receive eternal life (John 12:25). It's given to the just; those who walk in God's statutes and keep His judgments faithfully (Ezek 18:9). All this can only be accomplished by giving ourselves completely to Jesus Christ. When we give ourselves to God, we look for His mercy and are justified by His grace. We rest in His love and become heirs according to the hope of eternal life (Jude 21; Titus 3:7).

GOD'S REWARD FOR THOSE HE CALLS IN THIS AGE

The result of God's judgment of His people and the prophets—those who fear His name and love His appearing—is a great reward that can never be lost (Rev 11:18; Luke 6:35; Mark 9:38–41). Those who are troubled will find rest as we receive a crown of righteousness at His second coming (2 Thess 1:6–9; 2 Tim 4:8).

God rewards us according to our works. Those who want to be His must deny themselves, take up their cross, and follow Jesus. Those who desire to save their life must lose it (Matt 16:24–27; Rev 22:12; 1 Cor 3:8). Those who want to be first must be last and servant to all (Matt 19:30; Mark 10:31; Luke 13:30). Those who want to govern must serve (Luke 22:25–27). Those who desire to be great must submit to others. Jesus is the example for us all (Mark 10:41–45). He didn't come to be served but to serve and give His life a ransom for us. In human terms, the servant is the lesser, yet not with God, for Jesus is greater than any man, yet He served us. God has a special purpose for the people He calls in this age. To prepare us we must learn to serve others and humble ourselves before God (Mark 9:35; Luke 9:48).

Scripture tells us we will inherit the kingdom prepared for us from the foundation of the world (Matt 25:31–34; Luke 7:28). We will dwell in the house of the Lord forever (Ps 23:6). Jesus told us that when He leaves, He would prepare a place for each of us so that where He was we would also be (John 14:1–4). We will inherit all things and the earth, where God's kingdom will be firmly established at Jesus Christ's second coming (Ps 23:6, 25:13, 37:9, 22, 115:16; Matt 5:1–5, 6:9–10; Luke 22:29; Rev 21:7).

God has built a spiritual house, a royal priesthood, a separate nation, a chosen generation, and His own special people (1 Peter 2:5–10). We shall be named priests of the

Lord and people will call us the servants of our God (Isa 61:6). God will make some of us priests and Levites (a tribe of Israel dedicated by God to the service of the tabernacle and assisting the priests), some will be princes, and some will be kings (Isa 66:21; Rev 1:6). We will sit on thrones and live and reign with Christ in His kingdom here on earth for the thousand years we talked about in the resurrections chapter (Ps 45:16; Rev 3:21, 5:10, 20:4).

God's original intention for man was to rule over all of His creation on earth. He made us a little lower than the angels yet crowned us with glory and honor (Ps 8:3–8; Heb 2:5–8). God told Adam to fill the earth and subdue it; to have dominion over every living creature (Gen 1:28). At that time, God didn't give us authority over the environment. When God's kingdom is set up here on earth at Christ's second coming, the prophets and the people God is calling today will fulfill our destiny as God had originally intended. We will rule over all God has (Luke 12:42–44). With Jesus Christ as our king, all peoples will be subdued under us and the nations under our feet (Matt 25:21–23; Ps 47:3). God will give us power over the nations (Rev 2:26).

God's kingdom is a government, with levels of service. The example we are given comes from Israel as they traveled through the desert with Moses. Moses was trying to rule over every detail for the entire nation by himself. It was way too much for Moses to do on his own, so God sent his father-in-law, Jethro, to him to show him how to create levels of service, assigning rulers of thousands, rulers of hundreds, rulers of fifties, and rulers of tens (Ex 18:17–23). Jesus, in the parable of the ten minas (a sum of money), describes ten servants who each were given this sum of money and told to do business with it until the master returned. When the master returns, one servant made ten minas from what he was given, another made five minas from what he was given, and another servant didn't make anything from the money he was given but rather hid it away until the master came back. The master rewards the first servant with authority over ten cities and the second servant with authority over five cities (Luke 19:17–19). What Jesus is telling us through this parable is that if we are faithful in what He gives us in this life, our faithfulness will be rewarded with authority in His kingdom. The idea is that God will set up His government on earth in a similar fashion to how He established Israel, and we will rule with Jesus Christ, having authority over thousands, hundreds, fifties, and tens based on how faithful we were in this life with what we were given.

God's people will be honored with power over the nations to execute God's judgments and punishments on the nations; to bind their kings with chains and their nobles with fetters of iron; to execute on them the written judgment of God (Ps 149:5-9). We will judge the nations under the rule of Jesus Christ our king (Matt 19:28; Luke 22:29–30). Paul tells us that we will judge the world and the angels, so we should now be able to judge the things of this life (1 Cor 6:2–3). The purpose of us judging the people during the thousand-year period is to turn all people to God. As you can see, God is calling a people to Himself today for the special purpose of ruling with Him during the one-thousand-year reign of His kingdom here on earth. The rest of mankind will be given the gift of eternal life as they turn back to God in the second resurrection.

GOD'S WILL FOR ALL MANKIND

THE GRACE OF GOD

Before God called Paul, he was a violent man who persecuted the followers of Jesus Christ. He spoke of God irreverently and was ignorant of the power of God through Jesus Christ. God showed compassion toward Paul by giving him his ministry to unbelievers. By doing so, God was showing His patience through Paul as a pattern for the rest of us whom God would call to Himself (1 Tim 1:12–16). This favor and compassion God poured out on Paul is known as God's grace. Sometime later, Paul would describe his ministry as a testimony to the good news of the grace of God (Acts 20:24).

Any discussion on God's will needs to consider God's grace. God's grace is His unmerited favor. There's nothing—absolutely nothing—we can do to earn God's favor. God favors or loves us in spite of what we do. In Paul's case, he was sinning and rejecting Jesus Christ at the time when God decided to move in his life. Paul didn't earn God's favor. God loved Paul and chose Paul in spite of the sin in his life.

We are all God's children, so God loved us before we were born. Allow me to use an analogy, realizing that there's no human equivalent that matches God's love and unmerited favor for us. We typically talk of unconditional love for our children—loving our children without placing any conditions upon that love. There's nothing our child can do to earn our love. Even before our child is born we love him or her. As parents, we have expectations for our children, but no matter what they do, good or bad, we love them. Throughout their lives, our children may exceed our expectation or never live up to them. Either way, we love them; we love them unconditionally. That's a form of God's grace.

God extends His gift of unconditional love to us in that while we were still sinners and rejecting Him, Jesus Christ died for our sins (Eph 2:4–8; 1 John 4:9; Rom 5:6–8). He is God and sinless, yet He became a man and a substitute for our sin (2 Cor 5:21; Heb 2:9; John 1:16–17; Acts 15:11; 2 Cor 8:9; 2 Thess 1:11–12). God used His sacrifice as a replacement and total payment for our sins (Rom 5:15–21, 1–2). It's through this unconditional love that Jesus Christ has for us, that we are delivered from this evil age and have a renewed relationship with God (Gal 1:3–5). We receive the gift of the Holy Spirit because God and Jesus Christ love us (Jude 21). God's Spirit lives in us, washes us, and renews our relationship with Him (Titus 3:4–7). This comforts our hearts and gives us hope for everlasting life (2 Thess 2:16–17).

We are called to God by His unmerited favor (Gal 1:15–16). God has a plan for each of us, and He acts on that plan in His timing, regardless of what we've done or are doing at the time (Eph 1:5–6; 2 Tim 1:1). In fact, apart from God, we are all sinners that fall short of His glory, so God calls us according to His purpose and not because of anything we've done to merit that calling (Rom 3:21–26; 2 Tim 1:9). Anyone trying to win God's favor by their actions is bound by the law of God so their actions can only ever be counted as a payment on the huge debt they have for their sin (Rom 4:4–5). If we in any way consider that it's our actions that somehow make us right with God, we then boast in our self-righteousness (Rom 11:5–6; Eph 2:9; Rom 6:14). Our boasting brings glory to ourselves and not to our Creator God (Heb 13:9; James 1:17–18). Therefore, we need to always know that every good and perfect gift comes from God. That brings us to the next dimension of God's unmerited favor toward us—our walk with God.

The gifts given to us by God are according to the measure and favor God decides (Eph 4:7). As with our relationship with God, there's nothing we can do to earn God's gifts (Rom 12:4–8). Through God's unmerited favor, we are all given different gifts so that each of us may be sufficient and abundant in the work God has for us (2 Cor 9:8). Through God's unmerited favor we are enriched in everything (1 Cor

1:4–8). We are given wisdom and sound judgment and the knowledge of God's will (Eph 1:7–12). God teaches us how to live so our conduct reflects godly sincerity and wisdom. God gives us our ministries and the ability to witness with power (Acts 4:33; Gal 2:9; Eph 3:2–7). We are thankful and eagerly await the coming of Jesus Christ (2 Cor 4:15). As each of us receives gifts from God, we are to be good stewards of those gifts and use them for the good of others so that we will be found blameless at Christ's return (1 Peter 4:10; Titus 2:11–14; 2 Cor 1:12). All of this is done in us by God and because of His unmerited favor toward us.

Through God's love for us we receive help in our lives. Again, we cannot earn God's help. God will not allow us to be tempted beyond what we are able to handle and always provide the means for us to escape the temptation (1 Cor 10:13). God gives us the strength and the power to persevere (Eph 3:16; 1 Cor 15:10; Phil 2:13). God will allow us to suffer for a time but then will comfort and establish and strengthen us (1 Peter 5:10). God will keep us from stumbling in our walk with Him and build us up (Jude 24–25; Acts 20:32). God's unmerited favor and His unconditional love for us is all we need to prosper in life (2 Cor 12:7–10).

In the apostle's letters to the church, they frequently encouraged us to grow in unmerited favor and prayed for God's unmerited favor to be with us (Rom 1:7, 16:20; 1 Cor 1:3, 16:23; 2 Cor 1:2, 13:14; Gal 1:3, 6:18; Eph 1:2, 6:24; Phil

1:2, 4:23; Col 1:2, 4:18; 1 Thess 1:1, 5:28; 2 Thess 1:2, 3:18; 1 Tim 1:2, 6:21; 2 Tim 1:2, 4:22; Titus 1:4, 3:15; Philem 3, 25; Heb 13:25; 1 Pet 1:2; 2 Pet 1:2, 3:18; 2 John 3). Growth is absolutely a part of our walk with God, but it's not growth we initiate or can ever take credit for. We grow as we submit our lives to God, and He gives us spiritual gifts and helps and protects us. As God works in our lives, we learn more of Him and grow in our understanding of the wonderful, unmerited love God has for us. How fitting that the very last verse of the Bible is a wonderful promise to all mankind that the unmerited favor of Jesus Christ is with us (Rev 22:21)!

THE POWER OF GOD'S WILL

We know that God has no pleasure in the death of the wicked; that the wicked would be eternally separated from God in the second death. His desire is that all men turn from their wickedness and do what is right and pleasing before Him (Ezek 33:11, 19). God tells us that there is more joy in heaven over one sinner's repentance than over ninety-nine people who need no repentance. We are told that the angels of God are joyful over that one sinner repenting (Luke 15:7, 10). The proverb of the wasteful son drives this idea home for us in a very real way as we consider our own children, and how we would feel if one that was lost turned back to God. For all followers of Jesus Christ, it's our hearts desire that our children have a vibrant relationship with our Creator God, and we are joyous and blessed when that happens. How much more so with God!

It's also important to note that God does not put limitations or constraints on the timing of our turn from wickedness. There's nowhere in Scripture where it says that we must turn from our wickedness before we die or we're lost forever. As I mentioned before, we make those constraints, not God. God is dealing with each one of us in His timing, not ours.

God tells us that because of our disobedience to Him, He commits us to that disobedience. The purpose of committing us to disobedience is not to eternally condemn us but that He might have mercy on us; that we may know His compassion according to the multitude of His mercies (Lam 3:31–36; Rom 11:30–32).

When Jesus told His disciples that it was easier for a camel to go through the eye of a needle than for a rich man to enter the kingdom of God, they were all confused. Jesus told them that all things are possible with God (Matt 19:23–26; Mark 10:23–27). With God, nothing is impossible (Luke 1:37). The things that are impossible for man are possible with God (Luke 18:26–27).

God commits us to disobedience but does not cast us off forever. In fact, what God tells us is that He devises means to draw us back to Him so that we do not remain banished from Him (2 Sam 14:14). God tells us that He works three times to bring us back from eternal separation from Him (Job 33:29–30). For instance, we know from previous chapters that in this life we cannot excuse ourselves from acknowledging God because His creation cries out to us of His existence. We also know from Peter that God preaches the gospel to all those who are dead that they might live. The third time God works with mankind is during the judgment. So we see that God does work three times with the wicked to turn them back to Him. This idea is substantiated by Hosea when he tells us that God has torn us, but He will heal us. He has stricken us, but He will bind us up. After two days, God will revive us, and on the third day, He will raise us up, that we may live in His sight (Hos 6:1–3).

Jesus spoke a parable about a fig tree that produced no fruit for three years. The keeper of the vineyard convinced the owner to give him one more opportunity to care for it before deciding on its fate (Luke 13:6–9). Peter denied Jesus three times, yet Jesus told him to strengthen the brethren once he returned to Him (Luke 22:31–34). Jesus, wanting to fully restore Peter after His resurrection, asked Peter three times if he loved Him (John 21:15–19). What's important for us to hold onto in all this is that God does not give up on us. We are His children, and He will do whatever He deems necessary to turn us to Him.

We know that in our mortal state, we don't inherently have eternal life; that eternal life only comes from the indwelling of the Holy Spirit. Moreover, God designed us with the desire to live eternally so that we would strive for Him (Ecc 3:11). We can all see that in our lives. Most of us don't want to think of life just ending when we die. We hold onto the hope that there's something more, regardless of us being Christian or not. Those few that have been so completely deceived by Satan to think that this life is enough will probably change their attitude when they're standing before the throne of God.

God is able to subdue all things to Him (Phil 3:21). He tells us that every knee will bow to Him and every tongue confesses that Jesus Christ is Lord (Rom 14:10–12). God is clear that no one will escape showing Him this reverence and ultimately recognize Jesus as Lord and Savior. All those in heaven, all those on earth, and all those under the earth will confess that Jesus Christ is Lord, so no one should glory in His presence, but glorify Him (Phil 2:9–11; Ps 22:29; 1 Cor 1:29). I'd say that covers every single person who ever lived, don't you? Again, realize what these passages are saying. We already know that the condition for God to draw us back to Him is to recognize that Jesus Christ is our Lord and Savior. These scriptures clearly are telling us that there will come a time when every single person who ever lived will bow before God and confess that Jesus Christ is our Lord and God.

Since we all sin and fall short of the glory of God, judgment comes to all men, resulting in condemnation. However, through the righteous act of dying on the cross as an appropriate payment for us, the free gift comes to all men, resulting in being made acceptable to God through Jesus Christ (Rom 3:23, 5:18). Therefore, as in Adam all mankind dies a physical death, even so in Jesus Christ all shall be made alive—not just some, but all (1 Cor 15:22–28; 2 Cor 5:14–15; Rom 6:10; Heb 2:9, 10:10). God will draw all men to Himself and repair His relationship with all mankind.

Let's consider God's will and His sovereign power for a moment. Jesus submitted Himself completely to the will of the Father, even to the point of death (Matt 26:39, 42). God's will is for Jesus Christ to have authority over all flesh (John 17:2–3).

By God's will all things exist and were created. God spoke through His Word, Jesus Christ, and it was so (Rev 4:11). Everything that God created was good in His sight (Gen 1). By God's will His kingdom will come (Matt 6:9–10; Luke 11:2–4). These two truths are foundations of our beliefs as followers of Jesus Christ; that God created the heavens and the earth and has established a plan to draw mankind to Him that culminates with His kingdom ruling on the earth. Scripture tells us that these two pivotal events are the result of God willing them to happen. Our faith is established in the magnificence of God's creation. Our hope is confirmed in the knowledge that God's will is absolute (Luke 12:32).

Consider God's will for the church. Having predestined us to adoption as sons according to the good pleasure of His will, God chose His people to be special and blameless before Him in love (Eph 1:3–6). Therefore, nothing—death nor life, nor angels nor principalities nor powers, nor things present nor things to come, nor height nor depth, nor any other created thing— can separate us from the love of God (Rom 8:35–39). God is able to keep us from stumbling, deliver us from this present evil age and present us faultless according to His will (Jude 24; Gal 1:3-5). It's God who will prepare us completely; it is God's will that we be set apart (1 Thess 5:23-24, 4:3). He has begun a good work in us and will complete it (Phil 1:6). God gives us eternal life, and no one can snatch us out of His hands (John 10:28–29). God is greater than all. None of us who are truly His will be lost. God will raise His people up at the last day (John 6:38–45).

As God's people, we believe in all these promises and hold onto this hope because God tells us that this is His will for us, and we know God's sovereign power and authority. Do any of us not believe in the absoluteness of these promises? Why is that? It's because God tells us that it's His will for these things to happen, so we believe in them from the core of our being. It's important for us to grasp this understanding of God's will. God created all things and is more powerful than any of His creation. God will not tell us He wills something to happen and then not follow through. In simple terms, when God wills something to happen, it happens.

MANKIND'S RELATIONSHIP WITH GOD

God tells us He is for us, so no one can be against us. God delivered up Jesus Christ for all of us, so He, through Christ will freely give us all things. God tells us that He has mercy on those whom He wills and hardens whom He wills (Rom 8:31–33). No one can resist God's will, so it's not our place—being the creation—to question God, the Creator (Rom 9:18–21). The Father's command for Jesus was to bring everlasting life (John 12:49–50).

God is the savior of all men, especially those who believe (1 Tim 4:10). Did you catch that? God doesn't say He's the savior of only those who believe. In this passage, God makes it clear that not only does He save those who are His today, He saves all mankind. That's not to say that the conditions for being saved are not real. There's no contradiction here. What God is saying is that those who believe today are saved and the rest of mankind will also be saved when they turn back to Him.

God sent Jesus into the world to save the world. God so loved the world that He gave His only begotten son for us. Whoever believes in Jesus will not perish but have eternal life (John 3:14–21). Jesus said that He will draw all peoples to Himself (John 12:32). God's grace that repairs our relationship with Him appeared to all the nations (Titus 2:11). He sent His followers out to nurture those from all nations, telling them to preach His name and the good news about the kingdom of God to every person (Matt 28:19–20; Mark 16:15–16; Luke 24:47–48). God, in Christ is reconciling the world (whether things on earth or things under the earth) to Himself, having made peace through the blood of His cross (2 Cor 5:19; Col 1:19–20).

As we discussed earlier, Israel—for the most part—rejected God. Paul tells us that Israel will be accepted again if they do not continue in disbelief (Rom 11:23). If Israel's rejection allows for the reconciling of the world, their acceptance will be life from the dead (Rom 11:15). God further clarifies His will by telling us that all Israel will be saved; that God will take away their sins and make His covenant with them (Rom 11:25–29). We saw this same promise made to Israel in the prophecies of Ezekiel regarding Israel. Moreover, God tells us that it's His will that no one should perish but that all should come to repentance (2 Peter 3:9). It's God's desire that all mankind come to the knowledge of the truth and to be saved. God made Jesus Christ, who gave Himself a ransom for all to be the mediator between Him and us (1 Tim 2:4–6). Jesus echoed this same thought when He told us that it is not the will of the Father in heaven that one child should perish (Matt 18:11–14). We typically read over these verses without considering their meaning, after all, of coarse God would want all His creation to change their ways and turn back to Him. However, what God is telling us is that this is His will. The Creator God wills that all His children turn back to Him. These are profound statements—these are profound promises that God is making to all of His creation, and they are as absolute as His word is true.

John the Baptist, in preparing the way for Christ, said that all flesh would see God's restoration of our relationship with Him (Luke 3:4–6). When James and John saw that the Samaritans did not receive Jesus, they asked Him if He wanted them to command fire to come down from heaven and consume them. Jesus responded that He did not come to destroy men's lives but to save them (Luke 9:56).

Paul tells us that it's God's will that within His time frame, He will gather together all things in Christ, both in heaven and on earth (Eph 1:7–10). This was a mystery previously not understood by Israel and was something Paul needed to teach the early church. God is using His people to make known to all mankind the hope of our glory, Jesus Christ living in us. We preach and teach, and warn in all wisdom for the ultimate purpose of presenting every one of us perfect in Jesus, the Anointed One. (Col 1:26–28). From everything we've read it's clear that the writers of the New Testament and the early church understood the mystery that God's will for all mankind is to be members of His family.

However, it seems that this understanding was lost over the years and has become a mystery to us again. My prayer for all of us is that we can open ourselves to this truth and embrace the magnitude of God's love for His children.

God's word is clear. In the book of Revelation, John sees a vision of every creature in heaven, on earth, and under the earth, saying: "Blessing and honor and glory and power be to Him who sits on the throne, and to the Lamb, forever and ever!" (Rev 5:13). All God's creation will one day praise and worship our Lord and Savior, Jesus Christ.

GODS

When God created mankind, He created us in His image according to His likeness. Both man and woman were created in His likeness. God blessed us and placed us over His creation to have dominion over it (Gen 1:26–28, 31, 5:1, 9:6). Those God calls by His name He created for His glory (Isa 43:7; Ps 30:8–9). God tells us when He finished His creation it was good, but it wasn't complete. God's ultimate purpose for mankind is to be His children. Our destiny is to be sons of the Most High God (Matt 5:8–9, 45; Luke 6:35). We will be in God's house, within God's walls, and shine forth in the kingdom of our Father. We will be given names better than sons and daughters for we will be given everlasting names that shall not be cut off (Isa 56:5; Matt 13:43).

God makes very specific promises to His people that apply to all mankind as we turn to God. God has predestined us to adoption as sons by Jesus Christ Himself, and because we are sons, God will send forth the Spirit of His Son into our hearts, that cries out that He is our Father. Therefore, we are no longer slaves but sons, and if sons, then heirs of God through Christ (Eph 1:5; Gal 4:6–7). To everyone who believes in Jesus, God gives them the right to become His children (John 1:12, 14:23; Gal 3:26; Rev 21:7).

In God, we live and move and have our being for we are His offspring. Therefore, since we are the offspring of God, we ought not to think that the divine nature is like gold or silver or stone—something shaped by art and man's devising (Acts 17:28–29). Our ultimate destiny is to be gods and children of the most high (Ps 82:6; John 10:34–35).

THE TREE OF LIFE

When God placed Adam and Eve in the Garden of Eden, He provided every tree that was pleasant to the sight and good for food. There were also two trees there of significant importance to God: the tree of the knowledge of good and evil and the tree of life (Gen 2:9). God told them they could eat of any tree within the garden except the tree of the knowledge of good and evil. God warned them that in the day they ate of it, they would surely die (Gen 2:15–17).

We all know the story. The serpent (elsewhere in Scripture identified as the devil and Satan) deceives Eve, telling her that they would not die if they ate of that tree. He went on to tell her that God knew that in the day she ate of it, her eyes would be opened, and she would be like God, knowing good and evil (Gen 3:4). Satan's desire was to destroy mankind. We need to realize that prior to the creation of man, God had placed Satan as the ruler of this world, but he lost that position when sin was found in him (Ezek 28:11–15; John 12:31, 14:30, 16:8–11; Rev 12:9). As we've read earlier, man under Jesus Christ will replace Satan as ruler of this world, so Satan is doing everything in his limited power to stop God's plan. Satan is not trying to add to his demons or have more company with him in hell as some people think. His purpose as adversary is to try to stop God's plan by destroying mankind.

Think back to the Garden of Eden. The tree of life symbolizing eternal life was there to freely eat of. That was God's intention all along—to give eternal life to mankind. God placed no restriction on eating from that tree. The serpent, knowing this, didn't have Adam and Eve eat of it first and then deceive them with the tree of the knowledge of good and evil. He went directly to the tree that brought death to all mankind. It was at that point that God drove Adam and Eve out of the garden and placed angels and a flaming sword that turned every way to guard the way to the tree of life so that mankind could not access it anymore (Gen 3:17–24).

God created us to be His family; to have a close, intimate relationship with us. God wonderfully created us with a mind that can reason, think, create, and feel emotions. He gave us the desire to love and commune with each other, finding joy in our relationships with each other. He gave us the family unit to teach us how to serve and love and nurture each other. Moreover, God created us to be one with Him. We are incomplete apart from God. There's a beautiful picture the Garden of Eden paints for us. Adam and Eve had that close, intimate relationship with their Creator. God provided for all their needs. He would visit them and spoke directly to them. God brought all the animals to Adam to name, including him in His creative process. God would visit Adam and Eve in the cool of the day. Even after they had sinned, God affectionately called to them and clothed them when they were ashamed of their nakedness (Gen 2–3).

The tree of life not only represented eternal life, it represented that missing dimension in our lives today that can only be given as a gift from God when we turn our lives over to Him (Gen 3:22; John 6:63; Rom 8:11). The tree of life represents the Holy Spirit, and because of that it represents our renewed life as a part of God's family. Adam and Eve had a personal relationship with God before their sin, but their relationship never advanced beyond their physical existence. That's because they never received the part of them that would have completed them—the Holy Spirit. God was offering it freely to them, and then kept it from them because of their sin.

When Jesus healed the man at the pool of Bethesda, the Jews wanted to kill Him for working on the Sabbath. He told them He and His Father have been working until now (John 5:16-17). God has been working ever since mankind was driven from the garden to restore our relationship with Him. It was and is God's work. It was completed in Jesus Christ's shed blood; His death and resurrection from the dead. Because of God's work, all mankind has the hope of eternal life which God, who cannot lie, promised before time began (Titus 1:2).

OUR FATHER GOD

I have two boys that I love dearly. They mean everything to me. I was in love with them before they were born; while they were still a promise from God. From the moment they were born we had a connection. There was a bond formed that will last until I breathe my last breath.

While they were infants there were many difficult days for me (you Mom's out there will probably laugh at my laments). I can remember how I hated when the weekends came because I was responsible for getting up through the night and feeding the baby. My oldest son would sleep two hours and take over an hour and a half to finish his bottle and go back to sleep. The lack of sleep and late night infomercials really pulled me down. Then there was the colds, flu, ear infections, and asthma that would make the boys sick and cranky (Mom and Dad too). Yet what a joy to see the boys gain motor skills and develop personalities.

The young years were a time when Dad was pretty special. We would do things together and I could really see that the boys looked up to me and enjoyed spending time with me. I was blessed with the opportunity to mold their characters. It was during this time that I realized what it truly means to be Dad. If I was to be a role model for the boys I had to walk the talk. Issues like honesty, kindness, integrity, and building a relationship with God, all became a microscope for my life; magnifying my own weaknesses and struggles. Yet it was also a wonderful responsibility I was given by God. I was actually molding my son's characters. I found joy in the conversations we would have at the dinner table and at bed time. The times they would get in trouble and needed correction became additional moments to teach and mold them (even though it didn't seem that way at the time).

I learned that my son's and I weren't perfect (I know, what a revelation). They weren't the perfect model citizens I had envisioned and I wasn't a perfect role model, nor did I take advantage of every opportunity to coach that they presented me with. Sometimes I needed to let them make mistakes on their own and then live with the consequences. Too often, I bailed them out before the behavior was truly corrected. When I did correct them, my desire was to get everything out on the table quickly and then make sure our relationship remained in tact by letting them know I loved them. Sometimes my anger would get the best of me and I would do something I would soon regret. In those situations I would struggle to swallow my pride and apologize for letting my emotions get the best of me.

As young adults I failed my boys the most. As they were going through their High School years I failed to realize that even though they were pushing me away to gain independence, they actually needed me more than ever. My desire to allow them to express themselves and make their own decisions resulted in me not addressing behaviors that were dangerous to them. I gave in to their desires too often and didn't speak up when I should have. Thankfully, God has always been there to guide my son's and be a bridge for my inadequacies.

I realize as I get older and my boys have their own families that my role will change with my boys, but some things will never change. I will always desire what's best for them, I will always work to mold their character, and I will always be there for them. No matter what they do (good or bad) I will always be their Dad. They are a wonderful gift from God that I will always cherish.

Being a Dad has helped me to understand God's love and grace. We are all God's children, made in His image. He loved us before we were born. He works with each and every one of us to mold and shape our characters, so that we can enter into His family. He knows each of us better than we know ourselves. Therefore, His direction and instruction for each of us is unique and perfectly designed to turn us back to Him. His timing is also perfect. God works with each of us in His time. He is not constrained by time, chance, or any other physical constraint. This may be hard for some to grasp, but God's plan for each of us extends beyond death.

I use my relationship with my son's to demonstrate how God feels toward us but the reality of God's love is so much more far reaching than human love can ever be. God is perfect and His love for us and judgments of us are perfect. While

I gave in to my son's desires too often, God gives us exactly what we need, not what we request. I may be selfish with my time or react out of emotion but God is constant in His love and desire for us. I try to mold my son's into my image for them, yet God created each one of us with an outcome in mind that fits us perfectly. I may fail in molding my son's character but God will not fail.

There's another dramatic difference between me as a father and our Father, God. My son's have lived with me their entire lives. While they were young they depended on me for everything: food, shelter, clothing, education, emotional needs; everything. Can you imagine what it would be like to have your child from birth reject you and not desire a relationship with you? And then, when anything went wrong in their lives, they would curse you for not caring enough? And yet, that's what we've done to God. Adam and Eve's rejection of God pictures the rebellious spirit that has been within us ever since. God has allowed us to go our own way to teach us what the outcome of our decisions brings. Moreover, He chooses when and how He will eventually reveal Himself to each of us.

Enter grace. God's grace is amazing. Even though we reject Him, He will not reject us. Every single person documented in the Bible that God has had a close, intimate relationship with was chosen by God, not for anything they did, but because God chose them and gave them everything they needed to connect with Him. That's what grace is; being granted unmerited favor from God. There's nothing any of us can do to earn acceptance from God, apart from God. God chooses us in His timing and then provides everything we need to be acceptable to Him.

God's will is for all of us to be His family. He is so determined in His will for us that He came to us as a man, bore the shame and rejection of a people He called His own, died on a tree like a criminal, and yet was resurrected by the Father just as He promises to resurrect each and every one of us. When we finally come to a point (regardless of when it is) where we recognize our need for Him, and repent of our ways apart from Him, He gives us His Spirit and welcomes us into eternity with Him. Thankfully, we have a real, loving Father who is righteous and perfect in all His ways looking over us.

The book of Revelation sends a message of hope to all of us. To him who overcomes God will give to eat from the tree of life, which is in the midst of the paradise of God (Rev 2:7). God tells us that the leaves on the tree of life are for the healing of the nations (Rev 22:2). Blessed are those who do God's commandments that they may have the right to the tree of life and may enter through the gates into the city (Rev 22:14).

FINAL THOUGHTS

In the book of Luke, there's a parable about a lost son. The son wastes away his inheritance while the older son stays faithful to his father. The wasteful son eventually comes to his senses and turns back to his father. The father greets him with open arms and celebrates because his lost son has returned. Our focus is on the son who changed his ways and came back to his father. There's much joy in the father's house when the son who was lost comes home. This is how all the followers of Jesus Christ feel when someone turns back to God. Yet we see in the parable an older brother that's upset because he gave his entire life to serving his father, and when the younger brother returns from wasteful living, the father celebrates more for him than for the older brother (Luke 15:25–32). Who is the older brother? Why is he upset?

In the book of Matthew chapter twenty, Jesus tells us the parable of the laborers. In this parable, a landowner goes into the market and finds laborers throughout the day to work in his vineyard. Even though he contracted with laborers at various times of the day, he agrees to give each of them a day's wages for their work. Those who started working at the beginning of the day are upset, not because they worked a full day for a full day's pay, but they're upset because people who came at the end of the day were paid the same money for doing much less work. The landowner tells them he did them no wrong because he gave them what he promised and they agreed upon. He wished to give those who came later the same amount as he gave those who had come earlier (Matt 20:1–19).

We use these parables to illustrate how God calls people at various times in their lives, yet He offers eternal life to each as they accept that calling. You may become a Christian at the age of five and live your whole life serving God, or you may be called to God on your death bed, repenting of your sins and accepting Jesus Christ as your Lord and Savior. I agree with this line of thought, and it does show a measure of God's mercy and grace. God's desire is to give eternal life to everyone who comes to Him, regardless of when.

There is, I believe, a deeper meaning to both parables. The elder son is upset at the younger son being given a feast, yet he had abandoned the father for many years. The laborers who started work at the beginning of the day were upset that the laborers that came later received the same pay. In our traditional view of these parables, the elder son and the laborers who came at the beginning of the day would be followers of Jesus who have given most or all of their lives in service to God. They would be upset that those giving their lives over to Christ late in life receive eternal life just as they did. In our sermons, we usually point to these attitudes and encourage the listeners to change their thinking if they feel this way. However, this attitude toward people converted later in life is not a real emotion we find. People that have a heart for God, true followers of Jesus Christ, pray fervently, spread the good news, and witness all so that people will come to know God and turn back to Him. It's their heart's desire that all mankind would be saved, regardless of when. They are not bitter or angry at God for pouring out His mercy and love on the lost, because they all know that they were recipients of God's amazing grace as well. So then, who are these people in the parables?

I believe the deeper meaning of these parables applies to all mankind. The lost son and the laborers who begin their labors in the eleventh hour are those who have their place in the second resurrection. As we've seen throughout the Scriptures, God's desire is that all mankind have eternal life. Jesus Christ's death was for all mankind. God's mercy and grace applies to all His creation. What a wonderful plan God has to repair our relationship with Him!

Moreover, God is calling the firstfruits of His great harvest today for the special purpose of ruling in His kingdom during the one-thousand-year reign of Jesus Christ here on earth, but that does not make those chosen today any more special to God or put us in higher standing with God. When God tells us the first will be last and the last will be first, that concept has application on many different levels. All who are not called today and find themselves coming to know God in the second resurrection are His children, just like those called today are. All will have a special and unique purpose different from those called today but every bit as important to God.

Consider Paul and his calling again. Paul's charge by the Jewish leadership was essentially to eliminate the threat of this new sect following Jesus Christ using any means necessary. He had just consented to the stoning of Stephen and was headed to Damascus with orders to seek out and imprison any followers of Jesus he could find (Acts 7:57–60, 8:1, 9:1–2). To the early church, Paul was a wicked and feared man. When God decided to move in his life, Jesus showed Himself and spoke personally to Paul, and Paul was blinded for three days (Acts 9:3–9). God had a special purpose for Paul so He showed Himself in a powerful way to Paul. Just imagine how you (or anyone else) would react to God showing Himself to you in this way. Would your life be different? Would you change your ways? Would you commit to doing whatever God asked you to do?

Jonah tried to run away from the calling God had given him. When God said to go to Nineveh, he tried to go the opposite direction and escape to Tarshish (Jonah 1:1–3).

The consequence of Jonah tying to flee was that Jonah was swallowed by a large fish and kept there for three days (Jonah 1:17). Talk about a life-changing event! Needless to say, Jonah eventually did exactly what God had told him to do (Jonah 2:10–3:4).

For most—if not all of us that God has called—our walk with Him probably started in a much more subtle way. We all have different stories. It's always interesting to hear how God has worked in someone's life and brought about the changes that made them desire a relationship with Him. The point is that God works in unique ways with each and every one of us to serve His overall plan to establish His family.

Those of you who find yourselves upset with the ideas put forth in this book need to ask yourselves why. Was your situation prior to the time of your calling any different than those who die before coming to know their savior? Were you less of a sinner? Did you deserve a relationship with God any more than anyone else? Are you upset because you've done so much more work for God and deserve more? Are you someone caught up in works and believe that you had a choice, and chose God, which makes you more deserving of eternal life? Or is it that the principles put forward here are something you're unable to accept because they're so different than what you've been taught and been committed to for so long? I've heard ministers defensively proclaim that God doesn't give second chances, and the idea of second chances is not scriptural.

My hope for everyone reading this book is that you prayerfully realize that nothing needs to change in terms of your walk with God or your interaction with others—absolutely nothing. God's commands to love Him with all your heart and to love your neighbor as yourself still apply. Our commission is still to preach the way to all nations as a witness. We will continue to nurture those God is drawing to Himself. Our fundamental principles stay in place. The only thing that may need to change is our perspective on God's mercy and grace for His children. Isn't that why the apostles always encouraged the church's to grow in knowledge and the grace of God?

By growing in grace, we will develop a deeper compassion for others. The parable about the good Samaritan is very clear in telling us that everyone in the world, all of God's creation, is our neighbor; our brothers or sisters. Samaritans were considered to be no better than dogs to the Jews and yet when a man was in need the "religious" people walked by without lending a hand, while the Samaritan had compassion on the man in need and went out of his way to care for him (Luke 10:30–37). God wants us to have this same compassion for all mankind, not just the people in our congregation or denomination or who share our religious beliefs (1 Pet 3:8–9).

Later in his ministry, Paul would acknowledge how merciful God was toward him. He goes on to say that the mercy and compassion that God showed him would be an example for all of us (1 Tim 1:12–16). Any of us who have a relationship with God know how merciful and compassionate God was toward us. Given that, shouldn't we have the same compassion on others?

We were called to be a light and salt to the world remember. We are to have compassion on all mankind. Jesus came into the world to save all sinners, including you and me. It's through His mercy shown to us that others may see God as a merciful and loving God.

God's mercy and love for us—His children—is incomparable. As a father, I would give everything I have to ensure that my boys would grow up to be men of character. If it was totally in my control, I would work tirelessly to ensure that they knew and loved God. There is nothing else on earth that means more to me. How much more so with God toward us, His children! Praise God! May the grace of our Lord Jesus Christ be with you and all mankind.